All Things QUILTING

with **Alex Anderson**

From First Step to Last Stitch

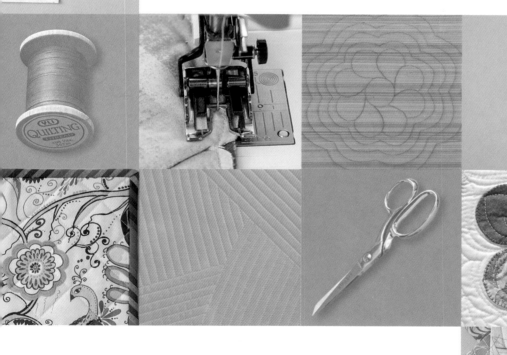

C&T PUBLISHING

Text copyright © 2015 by Alex Anderson

Photography and artwork copyright © 2015 by C&T Publishing, Inc.

Publisher: Amy Marson

Creative Director: Gailen Runge

Art Director / Cover Designer: Kristy Zacharias

Editor: Liz Aneloski

Technical Editor: Nan Powell

Book Designer: Christina Jarumay Fox

Production Coordinator: Freesia Pearson Blizard

Production Editor: Katie Van Amburg

Illustrators: Kirstie Pettersen, Tim Manibusan, Gretchen Schwarzenbach, Richard Sheppard, Rose Sheifer, Alan McCorkle, Jay Richards, and Jenny Davis

Photography: Diane Pedersen, Nissa Brehmer, Christina Carty-Francis, Luke Mulks, Sharon Risedorph, John Bagley, and Richard Tauber, unless otherwise noted.

Photo Assistant: Mary Peyton Peppo

Published by C&T Publishing, Inc., P.O. Box 1456, Lafayette, CA 94549

Library of Congress Cataloging-in-Publication Data

Anderson, Alex, 1955-

All things quilting with Alex Anderson : from first step to last stitch.

    pages cm

ISBN 978-1-60705-856-4 (soft cover)

1. Quilting. 2. Patchwork. I. Title.

TT835.A49353 2015

746.46--dc23

                              2014048647

Printed in China

10 9 8 7 6 5 4 3 2 1

DEDICATION

This book would not have been possible without the great community of quilting teachers who have inspired and educated us over the past several decades. Thank you, ladies and gentlemen, for elevating our craft to an unparalleled level of excellence. This book is dedicated to you and to those who are just now discovering the wonderful world of quilting. May this book be an integral part of your journey as you find your own personal voice in cloth.

ACKNOWLEDGMENTS

My sincere thanks to:

RJR Fabrics and Valori and Jean Wells of the Stitchin' Post (Sisters, Oregon), who graciously provided glorious fabric to work with;

BERNINA, for letting me play with and create using their *terrific* sewing machines;

Bob and Heather Purcell of Superior Threads, for their excellent products and their continued effort to educate the masses about the wonderful world of thread;

Olfa Products, for great tools to work with;

Carolie Hensley at The Cotton Patch (Lafayette, California) for her continued support;

Liz Aneloski at C&T Publishing, for being an editorial superstar;

Erica von Holtz, for her eagle eye;

Pam Vieira-McGinnis, "just for being there";

and last, but not least, Darra Williamson, who helps me keep my ducks in a row!

CONTENTS

INTRODUCTION:
A Few Words from Alex

One of the great things about quilting is that the creative journey never ends. The same can be said of the quilter's learning curve. There are loads of opportunities to expand our knowledge and a *zillion* ways to address the process. Since the 1997 publication of my book *Start Quilting with Alex Anderson* (now in its third edition), I've gone on to create an extensive series of "little books," each aimed at teaching a specific skill.

At a recent Quilt Market, a shop owner asked me if there were a book currently in print that encompasses *all* the subjects I've targeted in my little books. Bingo! Lightbulb moment! Perhaps the time had arrived for me to produce a "big book" of quilting—a perfect, one-stop resource guide for quilters. You now hold that book in your hands.

As I began to pull this "big book" together, I recognized that many things about the quilt-making process have remained the same, anchored by tried-and-true theories and techniques that have stood the test of time. They worked then, and they work now.

Quilting, however, is not a static endeavor. As with any craft, the materials and methods have continued to evolve. In this book, I've kept the best from my little books, while updating and expanding the information they contain. I've also added new material that I've never covered in my books before. My ultimate wish is that you consider this book your all-in-one, go-to place when seeking information to inform and improve your quilting.

I love meeting other quilters and am always flattered and humbled when I'm asked to autograph one of my books. I hope someday that I get to meet *you* and—should you present this book for me to sign—that your book shows all the signs of the love, wear, and tear that signal a well-used favorite.

Until we meet (and we quilters do get around),

ANATOMY
OF A QUILT

A quilt is like a sandwich. It has three layers:

The **quilt top** is made of fabrics (usually 100% cotton) cut in various sizes and then sewn together either by hand or machine to create the overall quilt design.

The **batting** is the filler between the quilt top and the backing. It forms the middle layer of the quilt sandwich. It is typically cotton, polyester, or a blend of both.

The **backing** is the bottom layer of the quilt sandwich. It can be made up of a single piece of fabric or pieced to achieve the appropriate width.

Quilting is the act of stitching all three layers together by hand or machine.

	— Quilt top
Batting	
	— Backing

The quilt sandwich

The following terms describe the various parts of the quilt surface.

The **block** is the basic unit of quilt construction. Many quilts are made up of multiple, repeated blocks, arranged in rows to form the **body** (or center) of the quilt.

When blocks or borders are **pieced**, individual fabric shapes are *seamed together* to create an overall motif.

When blocks or borders are **appliquéd**, individual shapes are *stitched on top of a base fabric* to create an overall motif.

Sometimes called lattice, **sashing** refers to fabric strips sewn between blocks to form a grid over the surface of the quilt center. In addition to separating the blocks, the choice of sashing fabric often allows these strips to create interesting secondary patterns, particularly when paired with **cornerstones** at each juncture.

A quilt's **border** acts as a frame. The border should make sense visually; that is, it should relate to or add something to the quilt's overall design. It might repeat or emphasize a key color, fabric, block, or other element in the quilt's body.

Sometimes a quilt will have more than one border. In addition to meeting the criteria above, multiple borders should be scaled in pleasing proportion to one another, as well as to the overall quilt. Along with sashing and cornerstones, you'll learn more about border options in Putting It Together: Settings and Borders (page 89).

Binding refers to strips of fabric used to finish and encase the edges of the quilt sandwich after the quilt has been quilted. You'll discover other possibilities for finishing the edges of your quilts in Finishing Touches (page 155).

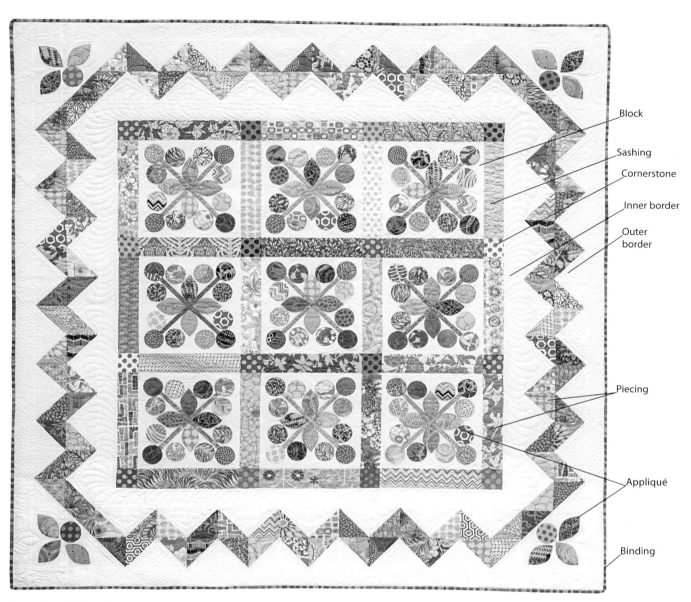

Block

Sashing

Cornerstone

Inner border

Outer border

Piecing

Appliqué

Binding

Flower Pops (56″ × 56″) designed and made by Alex Anderson, machine quilted by Angela Walters

Standard Mattress Sizes	
Crib	23″ × 46″
Toddler	27″ × 52″
Twin	39″ × 75″
Full	54″ × 75″
Queen	60″ × 80″
King (regular)	76″ × 80″
California king	72″ × 84″

IN THE SEWING ROOM

Whether you're blessed with the luxury of a dedicated sewing room or you must carve your creative space from a common area in your home, you'll want to incorporate certain physical characteristics and tools for a satisfactory quilting experience.

SEWING MACHINE

Let's start with the big boy: your sewing machine. The features you'll need to make a quilt are simple and few. Your machine should be in good working condition, with proper tension, an even stitch, and a good, sharp, size 80 needle.

If you plan to purchase a new machine—and I suspect you may as you fall in love with the quiltmaking process—do some research before you commit. Sewing machine companies love quilters and are eager to introduce new technologies that cut the learning curve and make our stitching easier. Consult the Internet to narrow your search, and then visit a dealer or two to test-drive and select the most comfortable combination of machine … and dealer.

You're making a big investment *and* establishing a long-term relationship with a professional who can provide valuable education and important service. Think of it as joining a family.

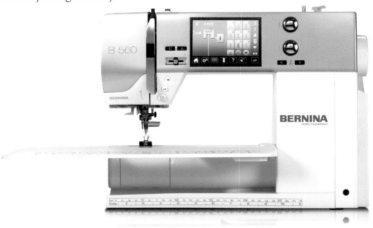

Shopping for a New Machine

I love my sewing machine (it's a BERNINA) for many reasons. Here are some of the key features I look for in a sewing machine:

- Needle up/needle down function: This feature allows you to stop stitching with the needle either raised or buried in the fabric. The latter position is especially useful for machine quilting; it enables you to hold your place as you stop to shift or pivot the quilt sandwich. You control this function either by hitting the base of the foot pedal with your heel (on some machines) or by pressing a button on the machine.

- Free-hand system or knee lift: In essence, this feature gives you another hand, enabling you to raise or lower the presser foot without removing your hands from whatever you are working on.

- Feed dogs: These can be lowered or dropped for free-motion quilting (see Free-Motion Quilting, page 152).

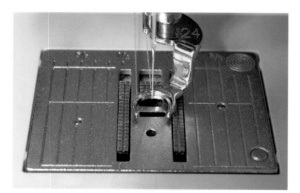

Feed dogs raised

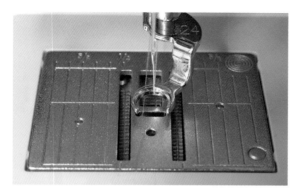

Feed dogs lowered

- Good, consistent tension that is easy to adjust.
- A variety of attachments—called **feet**—to suit the specific task at hand and the ability of the machine to accommodate them. A few basics would include a ¼" patchwork foot attachment for accurate piecing, an open-toe walking foot attachment for adding bindings and for straight-line machine quilting, an open-toe embroidery foot for machine appliqué, and an open- or closed-toe darning foot for free-motion quilting.

Open-toe walking foot

Open- and closed-toe darning foot

¼" patchwork foot

Caring for Your Machine

No matter how fine the machine, it will not perform at its best if you neglect to maintain it. If you spend lots of time stitching, and especially if you machine quilt, you're putting *lots* of wear on your machine. Clean and oil your machine regularly as the manufacturer directs—usually after every six to eight hours of stitching. Replace the needle after a day's sewing (for example, every seven to eight hours) or if you notice it becoming dull or burred. Finally, be sure to take in the machine every six to twelve months for professional service. Consider this preventive maintenance; mark it on your calendar so you don't forget.

YOUR PHYSICAL SETUP

No matter where you set up shop, you'll want your sewing space to be as comfortable, ergonomic, and efficient as possible. Here are some key physical aspects to consider.

Sewing table of the right height:

- For machine sewing, you want to be as comfortable as possible. I can't stress this enough!

- You'll want to be able to sit with your arms and legs at a 90° angle; at any other angle, you will place unnecessary strain on your neck, wrists, elbows, and knees. Position the table so that the quilt can't trail off the edge as it grows—for example, place it against a wall or in a corner. If this is not possible, surround the end of the table with chairs or enlist your height-adjustable ironing board to help support the quilt's bulk.

- If you haven't discovered them already, your machine dealer will probably introduce you to a variety of specially designed, commercially manufactured sewing tables. If you have the space and can spare the cash, you might want to give these a look-see.

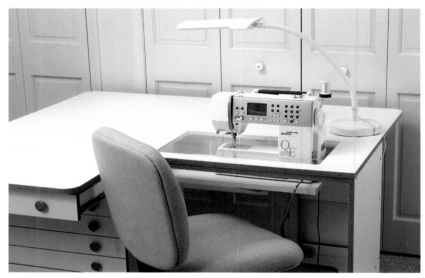

The ideal machine setup

---

tip

A slide-on acrylic tray makes a great alternative if you don't have the space or the money for a large, dedicated sewing table. This tray is a great way to adapt your machine for use on a regular table. This clever invention extends the bed of your sewing machine, enlarging the usable surface. It's useful for piecing, particularly as the body of your quilt grows larger, and it's a godsend for machine quilting. Look for a sturdy, well-constructed unit that aligns perfectly with the bed of your machine.

A slide-on tray is a great way to expand or adapt your work area.

Adjustable office chair: For maximum flexibility, select an armless chair that swivels and adjusts in height.

Lighting: Don't underestimate the importance of good lighting! The overhead light in your sewing room is probably not sufficient; supplement it with a portable task light that you can adjust and direct where the light is most needed. Position it so that there is no glare and so that it doesn't cast any shadows.

Cutting table: Some quilters keep a collapsible craft table in their workspace for cutting fabric. These tables work well for basting too, especially the waist-high variety made especially for sewists.

Iron and pressing station: Correct pressing is *very* important to making a successful quilt, and you'll be doing lots of pressing! The iron in your closet is probably just fine, but eventually you might want to purchase a super-hot steam iron. Some quilters reserve a separate iron just for use with their appliqué projects, particularly when these projects involve fusible web or spray starch. As for pressing surfaces, you'll want both firm (for preparing appliqué shapes and pressing pieced blocks) and soft (for pressing finished appliqué blocks).

Design wall: I can't imagine making a quilt without my indispensible, permanently mounted design wall. It's as essential to me as my sewing machine and rotary cutter. I use it for auditioning fabric choices and for experimenting with block arrangements and borders (see Putting It Together: Settings and Borders, page 89).

Seeing Stars (page 121) in progress on my design wall

Not everyone has the luxury of open wall space in the sewing room for a permanent design surface, but there are other options. One of my favorites is to cover one side of a large, 3′ × 6′ piece of foam core (available at most craft-supply stores) with flannel or felt, wrap the excess to the back of the board, and pin or staple to secure. You can prop this portable design board against a wall, door, or large piece of furniture while you're working, and then slip it under a bed for storage when you're not. While perhaps not as attractive or permanent, another option that will do in a pinch is to tape or tack a length of white cotton batting, felt, or flannel directly to the wall.

TOOLS AND NOTIONS

Quilters love gadgets, and every year more tools and notions are introduced to the quiltmaking world. Your first visit to a quilt shop or the quilting section of a fabric store can be overwhelming. There are many decisions to make when purchasing the necessary tools to get started. The following list includes the basics for a well-stocked sewing space. (Technique-specific tools will be addressed more fully in the appropriate technique chapter.)

If you've done any sewing at all, you probably already have some of these items on hand; others you'll need to purchase. Most important, gather the best-quality tools that you can afford and care for them properly—they will serve you well for years to come.

Thread: With so many delicious threads available on the market, it's impossible to expect your local quilt shop to carry them all, but it's likely that they'll carry what you need to get started. A good basic inventory should include threads suitable for piecing, appliqué, quilting, and basting. In many cases, quality 100% cotton thread, such as MasterPiece (see Resources, page 174), in neutral tans, grays, and creams, as well as in a few key colors, will be the perfect starting point.

If you expect to hand quilt, you may also want to stock up on hand-quilting thread, which is a little bit heavier than regular sewing thread. Some are made of 100% cotton, and others have a cotton-wrapped polyester core. As always, I suggest that you experiment to find your favorites.

In addition to color and fiber, thread comes in various weights, which is indicated on the spool with the "#" symbol. The higher the number, the finer the thread—so, for example, a #60 thread is finer than a #40 thread. A natural place to start would be in between, with a #50.

> **tip**
>
> Hooray! It's no longer essential to match fiber (the thread) to fiber (the fabric). So don't overlook *quality* polyester threads when building your thread inventory.

As your skill set increases to embrace machine appliqué and quilting, you'll want to bulk up your inventory with other options—for example, a quality invisible thread, such as MonoPoly (see Resources, page 174); jeans thread for machine buttonhole stitching; a high-end polyester, such as The Bottom Line (see Resources, page 174), for use in the bobbin; and so on. More on these threads, as well as specialty threads such as silks, rayons, and metallics, is addressed when we get to the appropriate techniques.

Needles: When purchasing needles for handwork—piecing, appliqué, or quilting—an important consideration is the size of the eye. Is it large enough to thread without difficulty? This feature can vary from brand to brand, so experiment to find not only which type but also which brand of needle suits you best.

Hand-quilting needles are called **betweens**. They're short and sharp and made specifically for hand quilting. At first, they may seem impossibly small, but you'll soon learn that the smaller the needle, the smaller the stitch. Like most other needles, betweens are sized by number: the larger the number, the smaller the size of the needle.

For the basic hand-appliqué stitch (see Basic Appliqué Stitch, page 79), I recommend that you start with size 11 sharp needle, which is long, slender, easy to maneuver, and easy to find. We'll explore other options in All About Appliqué (page 67).

For your machine-sewing needs, a good basic inventory should include sharps and topstitch needles.

Scissors: Keep three pairs of scissors on hand: one pair of sharp, 4"- to 5"-long shears with a sharp tip for cutting fabric; one for cutting paper and fusible web; and a small sharp pair for snipping threads, delicate cutting, and other small "housekeeping" tasks.

Rotary cutter (with extra blades): A rotary cutter is a rolling razor blade mounted on a plastic handle. Many different brands and sizes of rotary cutters are available. Here are the most common sizes and the tasks for which they are best suited:

- The small cutter (28 mm) is appropriate for small-scale or miniature projects and for cutting curves. You can cut up to two layers of 100% cotton fabric.

- The medium cutter (45 mm) allows you to cut up to four layers of 100% cotton fabric. If you start with just one cutter, this is the one I recommend.

- The large cutter (60 mm) can handle up to six layers of 100% cotton fabric. It's a must for the dedicated quilter who does lots of cutting.

If you have physical issues (such as arthritis) that restrict the use of your hands or arms, try a cutter with an ergonomically designed, curved handle. These cutters feature a comfortable grip and a simple-to-control safety latch.

Experiment until you find the brand and size that *you* like best and that best suits your needs.

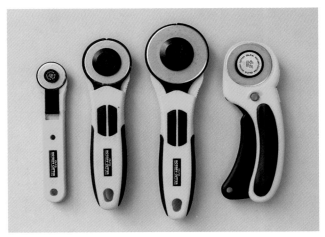

28 mm, 45 mm, 60 mm, and ergonomically designed Olfa rotary cutters

One last note on the rotary cutter: this is a sharp and—if handled or maintained improperly—potentially dangerous tool. More on safety and maintenance when we get to cutting (see Safety First, page 36, and Basic Rotary-Cutting Technique, page 37).

Rotary mat: This self-healing composite mat must be used when you're cutting with a rotary cutter. I recommend a gridded mat in either a medium (18″ × 24″) or large (24″ × 36″) size. The medium one is great for starting out or taking to class. The larger one is even more versatile. I suspect that eventually you'll want both. Keep the mat out of direct sunlight and never leave it in a hot car, as heat will cause the mat to warp.

Rotary rulers: These thick acrylic rulers are made especially for use with the rotary cutter and mat. Typically, they have ⅛″ increments marked in both directions, as well as angles marked for cutting 45° and 60° angles. They are substantial enough not to be "sliced" when used with the rotary cutter. To start, I recommend a 6″ × 12″ rectangular ruler for cutting strips and shapes and a square ruler for sizing blocks and squaring corners.

Other rulers: Though not for use with a rotary cutter, you'll also want to keep a thin, 2″ × 18″ acrylic, gridded, see-through ruler on hand for checking seam allowances, marking grids for quilting, and other utilitarian sewing-room tasks.

Pins: Don't skimp on these! My favorites are extra-fine (1⅜″/0.50 mm) glass-head pins. I use them for piecing and appliqué. They're a bit pricey but well worth the investment, especially if you stock up when the good ones go on sale. Avoid large, bargain-brand quilting pins for piecing and appliqué; not only can they get in your way and tangle with your thread, but also their thickness can throw off the accuracy of your seams.

You'll also want pins to use for temporarily securing the layers of your quilt sandwich for basting in preparation for hand quilting. (Eventually, you'll replace them with thread.) For machine quilting, rustproof size #1 safety pins are a good choice. The colored ones are extremely pliable, easy to see … and fun!

Marking tools: There are lots of options for marking on fabric, but my personal favorites are silver pencils (there are many brands available) and extra-hard-lead mechanical pencils. If the pencil says "verithin" it just means a very thin lead. These simple tools allow me to mark a nice, fine line;

they show up on most fabrics; and all of their marks are fairly easy to remove with gentle washing. Another popular option is Pilot's FriXion pen (see Resources, page 174), which doesn't require washing to remove. A water-soluble pen can be useful for marking quilts for machine quilting (although I avoid this type of marker for hand quilting, where it may leave a residue that's tough to quilt through). If you use a water-soluble marker, be sure to *follow the manufacturer's instructions carefully*, and be aware that you must be willing and able to immerse the finished quilt in cold water to remove the markings. The markings from these pens are also very sensitive to heat, so never press the marked quilt top until the markings have been removed.

> ### tip
>
> *Always* test your intended marking tool on a sample of your fabric before marking to make sure the marks come out.

Stiletto and seam ripper: A stiletto is a sharply pointed tool that you'll find helpful for coaxing turn-under allowances on appliqués and for controlling small pieces as you feed them through the sewing machine. A seam ripper … well, even a seasoned quilter needs one from time to time. My 4-in-1 Essential Sewing Tool by C&T Publishing (see Resources, page 174) includes a stiletto and a seam ripper, plus a pointed end for turning under fabric edges, as well as a handy pressing tool.

4-in-1 Essential Sewing Tool

¼″- and 1″-wide masking tape: This tape comes in handy for marking straight lines and grids for quilting, taping layers in preparation for basting, and many other basic sewing-room tasks. Another option is blue painter's tape; although it comes in a limited number of widths, it doesn't leave residue as masking tape is sometimes wont to do.

Fine-lead mechanical pencil and eraser: You'll use this versatile pencil for dozens of sewing-room tasks. As to the eraser: we all make mistakes once in awhile!

Black, permanent, felt-tip pen: You'll find many uses for a fine-tipped permanent marker in the sewing room.

Heat-resistant template material: For shapes that must be traced multiple times, both for piecing and appliqué, it's a good idea to make a template from sturdy material. While cardboard or card stock will work, a much better choice is the translucent template plastic available at your local quilt shop. Choose a heavier, heat-resistant variety for appliqué, particularly for circles.

Lightbox or light table: A lightbox provides a light source that will enable you to transfer your quilting motifs onto the quilt top and to trace and position appliqués. Any flat, clear, backlit surface will work. Commercial lightboxes are available, but I prefer a larger surface to work on. My light "box" is an 18″ × 36″ piece of ¼″-thick, clear Plexiglas. When it's time to trace, I set it between two chairs and place a lamp on the floor beneath it. If you have a dining room table that extends with leaves, consider getting the Plexiglas cut a couple of inches larger that the size of the leaves. Extend your table, substitute the Plexiglas for the leaves, and place a lamp on the floor beneath. You can also substitute a sunny window or place a lamp or flashlight beneath a glass-topped table.

You may have noticed an obvious omission in this description of the well-stocked sewing room: fabric! That's because it gets a chapter all its own, beginning on the next page. …

FABRIC AND COLOR:
CHOOSE IT
AND USE IT!

A huge common element that binds quilters together is our passion for fabric. No surprise here: fabric is our lifeline to creativity.

FABRIC GRAIN

When fabric is produced, the threads are woven in two directions, creating a lengthwise and crosswise grain. The long, finished edges of the fabric are called the **selvages**.

The lengthwise and crosswise grain is called the **straight of grain**. The lengthwise grain runs parallel to the selvages and has little, if any stretch. The crosswise grain, which runs across the fabric from selvage to selvage, has a *little* stretch. The **bias**, which runs diagonally across the fabric in any direction, has lots of stretch. Because of this, handle any bias edges— whether cutting them, sewing them, or pressing them—very carefully to avoid distortion.

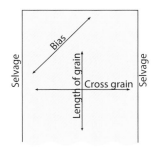

■ LET'S SHOP!

New fabrics continue to appear in the marketplace, and we quilters do love the new stuff! Colors and styles come and go, and it's always a good idea to take advantage of the opportunities when we see them. An infusion of even a few trendy colors and prints can add freshness to your quilt.

I'm always on the lookout for fabrics to expand and enrich my stash, and when I find something I like or that I know will fill a gap in my collection, I buy at least ⅓ yard. If I find a print that has the potential to become the foundation for a quilt—for example, a promising focus fabric (page 27)—I guesstimate enough for a border and then add an additional ½ yard, just in case. (If nothing else, I know I can use the yardage for backing.)

When determining your own shopping guidelines, budget and storage space will, of course, come into play, as will the size quilts you usually make. A quilter who leans toward king- or queen-sized projects will probably buy more fabric—either in variety or quantity—than one who rarely makes anything larger than a wall quilt.

A FEW WORDS
ABOUT QUALITY

For the most part, I recommend that you work with the best 100% cotton fabric available from your local quilt shop. Fabric of lesser quality—for example, with a looser weave, with a lower thread count, or the result of improper processing— might ravel, stretch, or distort, making accurate piecing and smooth appliqué difficult, if not impossible. A great deal of work goes into making a quilt, and your time is worth the best materials available. I would rather have five pieces of quality fabric than twenty pieces of lesser quality.

THREE KEYS TO SUCCESSFUL FABRIC SELECTION

Whether you're gathering fabrics for your very first quilt or you're a long-time quilter working on building a healthy fabric collection, the same basic principles apply. Aim for a good mix of color, value, and character of print.

Color

When we speak of a color, we're speaking of that color's *entire family*—and color families can be quite large. They include all the lights and darks, tints and shades of that particular family.

Meet the Red family!

Don't be afraid to open yourself to *all* the colors available to you, not just the ones that you love and that you've always been drawn to. As you continue to grow your fabric stash, keep an eye out for the colors that are missing from your collection and make a note to hunt them down next time you head to your favorite fabric source. Your future quilts will love you for it!

If you look at old quilts, you'll often find colors, or combinations of colors, that would never cross your mind as candidates for your next quilting project. Our foremothers (and, occasionally, forefathers) were fearless; they worked with rich red, electric blue, bile green, bubblegum pink, citrus yellow, cheddar orange—sometimes all in the same quilt—and we're still admiring these quilts more than 125 years later.

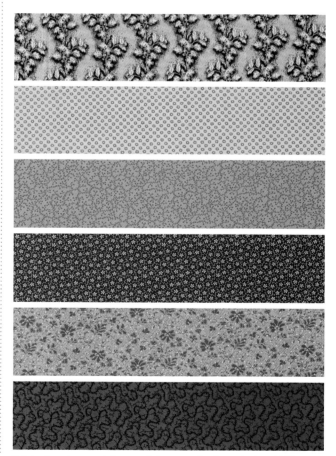

Fabrics in colors reminiscent of vintage quilts from the late 1800s

WORKING THE WHEEL

When I'm stumped for a color scheme, feel my palette would benefit from the addition of another color (or colors), or wonder if the colors I'm considering will play well together, I look to the color wheel. It's a great guide for determining successful color relationships, especially when you're expanding your horizons to work with colors you might not have worked with before.

Here are a few basic color schemes that you can draw from the color wheel.

Monochromatic: This color scheme showcases a single color family in all its glory—for example, a blue color scheme can include blues from the palest baby blue to deep, rich navy.

Complementary: This color scheme is built around two color families that appear opposite each other on the color wheel, such as red and green.

Triadic: This color scheme is built around three color families that are equally distant from each other on the wheel, such as yellow-orange, red-violet, and blue-green. To find a triadic color scheme, start with a single color on the wheel, and—moving clockwise—skip three colors, select the next, skip three more, and select the next color. Skip another three colors and you're back to your starting point, creating a perfect triadic color scheme.

Analogous: This color scheme is made up of neighbors on the color wheel and can include three, four, or more side-by-side color families. This is one of the easiest and most relaxing schemes to work with, as each color contains some element of its immediate neighbors, and the colors flow seamlessly, one to the next.

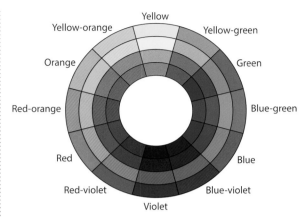

Color wheel

Monochromatic color scheme

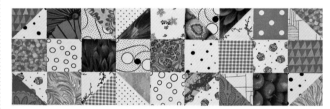

Complementary color scheme

Triadic color scheme

Analogous color scheme

Value

Value refers to the relative lightness or darkness of a fabric. You'll want to be certain that you have a good range of values—light to dark—of every color in both your quilt and your stash. A range of values is what transforms a color into a color family.

The key word in the definition of value is *relative*. You can't tell how light or dark a fabric is when you look at it by itself. It all depends upon the other fabrics that surround it in the block or quilt.

For example, in a Star block, the star points define the star image. If you place the fabric with the strongest contrast in value—say, the darkest fabric—in the "point position," there'll be no missing your intent. On the other hand, place that dark fabric in the center of the star, and that's where your eye will go. Set a bunch of these blocks together, and your Star quilt will read as a sea of big, dark squares.

Even though some of the star-point fabrics in these blocks are not super dark, they are always *relatively* darker than the fabrics I used for the star centers and background, so the stars come shining through.

Character of Print

Character of print refers to the figures or motifs that appear on a printed fabric. (Some quilters call this "visual texture"—same thing.) As with color and value, you'll want your quilt and your fabric collection to include a good mix of prints. Here are some examples.

Florals

Plaids

Dots

Feathers and paisleys

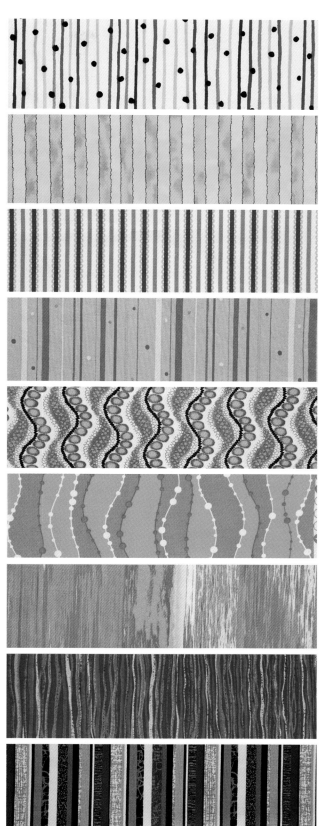

Stripes

Picture prints

Organics/foliage

Nature's bounty

Swirls and twirls

Geometrics

tip

Don't be afraid of large-scale and otherwise unusual fabric designs. You'll be cutting these fabrics into small pieces, and the results can be surprising. A window template, tailored to the size and shape of the piece you'll be cutting, will give you a good preview.

A window template gives you a unique perspective on large-scale or otherwise unusual prints.

▪ ADD SOME SPARKLE

Before we move on, I want to put in a word for what I call sparkle and bridge fabrics.

Sparkle fabrics *are typically monochromatic prints that include the complete range of value—light to dark—of their particular color family; sometimes they include bits of white as well. You'll love the crispness these lively prints add to your quilt.*

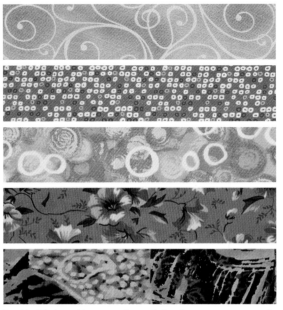

Sparkle fabrics add personality and visual texture to your quilt.

Bridge fabrics *are also usually monochromatic prints that have several color variations from within a single color family. These fabrics ease the transition when you're using many variations of one color family within your quilt. Notice how the fabric used for the top bar shown below pulls all the different colors within the family together.*

The fabric in the top bar is the bridge fabric.

ALTERNATIVE STRATEGIES FOR CHOOSING FABRICS

Fabulous Focus Fabric (or Favorite Designer)

A focus fabric is a multicolored, often large-scale print that you can build a color scheme—and a quilt—around. In short, the fabric designer has done the heavy lifting for you. Study the colors in the focus fabric, pull a variety of fabrics in those colors from your stash, check that they include a good range of values and character of print, and you're ready to go.

Occasionally, a designer comes along whose fabrics just speak to me, and I find myself adding more and more of that designer's pieces to my stash. Over time, that area of my collection grows to include "vintage" pieces from that designer's various fabric lines, as well as his or her newest creations. My guess is that you have your favorite designers (or fabric lines) too … and they make another great starting point for a super quilt. *Seeing Stars* (page 121) is a good example of a designer-inspired quilt. In this case, the designer was Kaffe Fassett.

If you're building your quilt around a focus fabric, purchase enough for a potential border. If you don't use it there, you can use it for backing.

Baskets (56″ × 56″) designed and made by Alex Anderson, machine quilted by Diana Johnson. My focus fabric for this quilt was the large-scale multicolored print that I used for the border.

Capture a Style or an Era

Given my love for vintage quilts, it's not surprising that some of my favorite quilts are those that replicate the look or style of a particular time period. With so many luscious reproduction fabrics available, it's fun—and easy—to make a quilt that looks as though it were fashioned in the nineteenth century or created during the height of the 1930s quilt revival.

Wheels and Fans (76″ × 76″) designed and made by Alex Anderson, hand quilted by Amish quilters. This quilt was built around my treasured stash of feedsacks and 1930s reproduction fabrics.

CARING FOR YOUR FABRIC

You've got your fabric home. Now what do you do with it? Given its importance, it's no wonder that we have so many questions when it comes to the proper care of our beloved fabrics.

To Prewash … or Not?

Perhaps first and foremost is the question: to prewash or not? I can guarantee that you'll get a *very* different answer depending upon whom you ask; be assured, there is not a gentle divide between "yes" and "no." The sentiment is usually—shall I put this delicately?—very strong one way or the other, and either way, the individual responding can offer you some very clear-cut reasons for the response. That said, here are my thoughts regarding this sensitive hot spot in the land of quilting wisdom.

In general, my philosophy is to prewash, and here's why:

- At its first washing, 100% cotton fabric has a tendency to shrink a bit. Better it shrinks before than after it goes into your quilt.

- Dyes from darker fabrics have been known to migrate (or bleed) into lighter fabrics. Ouch!

- Fabric can gather dust while sitting on the quilt shop's shelves or while waiting in your stash. It is also treated with various chemicals during the production process—chemicals I'd prefer not to inhale or touch.

Still on the fence? Consider how the finished quilt will be used. Chances are, if you're making the quilt for use on a bed or by a child, at some time that quilt will need to be laundered. Best to wash the fabrics now so there are no problems later. This is even more critical if you are giving the quilt as a gift and have no control over its future "life." Prewash now and tuck instructions for aftercare into the box with your quilted gift (see Caring for Your Quilts, page 170). If your quilt is purely decorative and will likely never require immersion, you may decide to skip the suds.

Some quilters prefer the crisp feel of unwashed fabric and argue that this crispness is lost when the fabric is laundered before being cut and sewn. Here's a solution. If the fabric seems excessively "limp" after washing, use a *light touch* of spray starch or sizing on the fabric when pressing it afterward. Keep in mind that when you make this choice, you're also making the commitment to wash the finished quilt to remove any product residue.

TIPS FOR (FABRIC) LAUNDRY DAY

Here are some tips for prewashing your fabrics before using them in your quilt.

- *Completely unfold the fabric before placing it in the sink, tub, or washing machine.*

- *Always wash light and dark fabrics separately.*

- *Wash your fabrics using the same water temperature and with the same gentle detergent you would use for your best cotton clothing.*

- *Leave the selvages intact until you've washed the fabric and make a small snip in each corner of the piece before popping it into the washing machine. This helps keep the edges of the fabric from raveling as the fabric is agitated.*

- *Use a small bag, suitable for laundering delicate lingerie, for washing especially small pieces of fabric.*

- *Remove fabrics from the dryer as soon as the drying process is complete. (Some quilters even remove the fabrics while still slightly damp.) This makes pressing so much easier!*

- *Although hand-dyed fabric goes through many immersions in the dyeing process, always test-wash your purchased hand dyes at home before you use them. Water is treated differently in different places, and fabric that ran clear for the dyer may still give off color in your water. Better to be safe than sorry!*

■ TROUBLESHOOTING: TRIAGE FOR BLEEDING FABRIC

If you choose not to prewash, you should at least test your fabric for colorfastness.

Place a 2" square of test fabric in boiling water. If the color runs off into the water, repeat the process. If it no longer bleeds, you can use it in your quilt, but you will need to prewash the remainder to feel confident in using it. If it continues to discharge color after multiple soakings, save it for a project that will not be laundered.

The experience of having the colors in unwashed fabric run (or bleed) when the finished quilt is laundered—or even dampened or sprayed to remove any marking— defines the word heartbreak. Even

if you've never experienced it, I'm sure you've heard the sad, sad stories. I am particularly cautious of reds and red-based colors, such as purple, that have a lot of red in them, but I have also learned to be cautious of even more "innocent" colors.

Some wonderful products on the market can help resolve the problems of bleeding fabric, either in the pre-wash stage or in a finished quilt.

Synthrapol *releases and suspends excess dye molecules in the water so that they pass safely down the drain. This product is particularly great for laundering hand-dyed fabrics. It also can be effective when laundering a finished quilt, keeping loose dye particles in suspension so they don't creep into other areas of the quilt.*

Retayne *is used to set dye, primarily in commercial fabrics. It increases the size of the dye molecules so they get "wedged" into the fiber. You might want to consider prewashing your quilting fabrics with Synthrapol and then using Retayne to set the color in the final wash.*

*Many quilters swear by **Shout Color Catchers**, which are readily available at supermarkets where you typically find laundry products. When used during the washing process, these "magic sheets" act like a sponge to attract and soak up excess dye in the wash water.*

My advice? Experiment with the options available to see which products you like best and which work best for you in a given situation.

WHERE AND HOW TO STORE IT

There are a million ways to store fabric; however, first and foremost, it should be kept away from a light source—natural or artificial—to avoid fading. Second, your fabric should be easy to access. If it's an effort to pull out your fabric to play with, most likely you won't bother.

I removed the doors from my sewing-room closet, purchased a spring rod, installed pull-out wire baskets, and made a split curtain to protect the fabric from the light.

I sort my fabrics by color families, with odd fabrics that don't fit a family, such as multicolored focus fabrics, novelty prints, or plaids, each stored in a separate bin. I fold the fabrics and store them on end, which makes them easy to sort through to find just the right one. I use an old suitcase as a catchall for my smallest scraps.

Another option is to purchase lidded boxes from a business or home storage company, label the boxes, and use these for storage. Avoid plastic bags; you want your precious fabrics to breathe.

You can sort and store fabrics by color, by style, by era (nineteenth-century reproductions, 1930s prints), by use (focus or border fabrics), or even by designer.

DRAFTING: HAVE IT YOUR WAY

Have you admired a quilt pictured in a book or magazine, only to find that the pattern is for a 9″ block when you'd rather make it in a 12″ version? Have you searched in vain for the quilt block pattern that you spotted at a museum exhibit or an out-of-town quilt show? If you can draft your own patterns—no problem!

The ability to draft your own patterns is probably one of the most valuable—but overlooked—skills that you can acquire as a quiltmaker. Despite what you may think, it's a very simple process. Time to take charge!

The single most important word to keep in mind is *accuracy*. A little extra care at this point can result in a quilt that lies flat and hangs straight—a joy to behold and a pleasure to construct.

Take your time and work in good light. Most of all, enjoy the sense of freedom that drafting your own blocks can bring.

WHAT YOU'LL NEED

- **Sharp (or mechanical) pencil**
- **Pencil sharpener** (*optional*)
- **Eraser**
- **Graph paper:** Paper gridded with four or eight squares to the inch is best for drafting quilt blocks. (I like the kind with darker lines to mark off the inches.) This allows you to work in familiar ¼″ and ⅛″ increments. Sometimes you can find this paper in convenient 12″-square pads, designed by and for quilters, at your local quilt shop. Gridded graph paper is also available in blotter-sized pads at office supply stores—perfect for drafting larger blocks. Be sure that the grid is marked accurately before making your purchase.

- **Drafting ruler:** This is *not* the place to use your thick rotary rulers, which are good for cutting but not for drafting! An accurate, 12″ or 18″, cork-backed metal ruler is ideal. (The cork keeps the ruler from shifting and slipping.) Typically made for architectural drafting, these rulers are clearly marked with ¼″, ⅛″, and even ¹⁄₁₆″ increments and tend to be extremely accurate.

- **Compass:** You'll need this for drafting simple eight-pointed stars and hexagons. You don't need one with bells and whistles. The simple, expandable version you used in school will work just fine. Just make sure it's sturdy enough to hold the desired measurement without slipping.

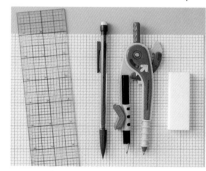

Basic drafting tools

DRAFTING BLOCKS BASED ON GRIDS

A grid is a square subdivided into small, equally sized squares. If you look closely at many popular quilt blocks, you'll notice that many of them are based on grids. Sometimes the grid is divided into four, nine, or sixteen equal squares. As you can see, some of the squares are further subdivided into smaller squares or triangles.

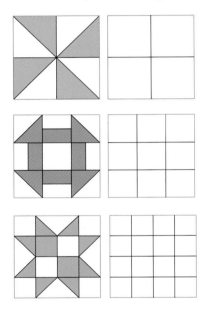

Step one in drafting a grid-based block is to draw the appropriate grid. Let's use the Churn Dash block as an example. If you look closely, you'll see that Churn Dash is equally divided into nine squares: three across by three down. To begin drafting this block, you'll need to draw a nine-patch grid.

Churn Dash = nine-patch grid

Next consideration: How large should you make the grid? Unless there's a specific size you need to fit a specific quilt plan, it's easiest to size blocks to correspond mathematically with the appropriate grid. Since Churn Dash is a nine-patch grid (three squares across by three squares down), a good choice is to create a finished block of 6″, 9″, or 12″—all evenly divisible by three. For this example, let's assume a 9″ finished block.

1. Using a sharp (or mechanical) pencil and an accurate drafting ruler, carefully draw a 9″ square on a sheet of gridded graph paper.

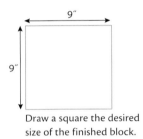

Draw a square the desired size of the finished block.

2. Measure and then carefully divide the 9″ square into a grid of 3 equal-sized squares across by 3 equal-sized squares down. In this case, it's easy to determine that each square in your grid should measure 3″.

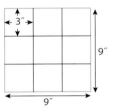

Divide the large square into 9 squares, each 3″ × 3″.

3. Beginning in the upper-left square of your grid, ask yourself, "What must I do on my grid to make this square correspond to the upper-left corner of the Churn Dash block?" In this case, you'll divide the square diagonally into 2 half-square triangles. Move across the grid to the next square, repeating, "What must I do …?" After dividing that square into two equally sized rectangles, move on, until you have systematically transferred all 9 squares. The Churn Dash has appeared on your grid. Done!

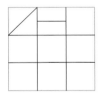

Transfer the design to the corresponding grid.

If, after drafting the block, you decide a 6″ block might make a better option, just repeat Steps 1–3, but this time starting with a 6″ square. In this case, the grid will be composed of 9 squares 2″ (6″ ÷ 3 squares = 2″). The rest of the drafting process remains the same.

DRAFTING NON-GRID-BASED BLOCKS

While many familiar blocks fall into a recognizable grid, some do not. One popular exception is the Eight-Pointed Star block.

Drafting an Eight-Pointed Star

At first glance, it may be difficult to tell the difference between a nine-patch star, such as the Ohio Star, and the basic Eight-Pointed Star, yet there is a key difference.

In the Ohio Star, the measurements between points A and B and between points B and C are identical. This is because this nine-patch star is based on a grid composed of nine squares of equal size.

Ohio Star = nine-patch grid

The Eight-Pointed Star, however, is based on an octagon, an eight-sided shape with all sides equal. The distance between A and B is equal to the distance between B and D but not to the distance between B and C as in its nine-patch cousin. Therefore, a different basis must be used to draft the Eight-Pointed Star.

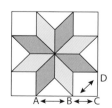

The Eight-Pointed Star is based on an octagon.

Here, the measurement from A to B = the measurement from B to D.

Don't be intimidated by the octagon ... or by the compass you'll use to divide the block. Just follow along, step by step.

1. Using a sharp (or mechanical) pencil and an accurate drafting ruler, carefully draw a square to the desired size of the finished block.

2. With a light hand, divide the square in half both vertically and horizontally, and then again on the diagonal in both directions. The center point will now be clearly visible.

Divide the block vertically, horizontally, and diagonally.

3. Open your compass so that it spans the exact distance from one corner of the block to the center (XY in the diagram below). Without changing the measurement, pivot the compass from the corner to the left and the right, making pencil marks where the compass crosses the block perimeter (Z in the diagram). Repeat from each corner until there are 8 marks, 2 on each side.

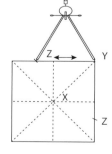

4. Beginning at the top left and moving clockwise, label the marks A and B on each side. Use your ruler to draw vertical and horizontal lines to connect all A's with the B's on the *opposite* side of the block.

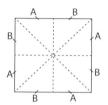
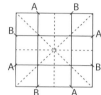

5. Connect each A with the "long distance" B on the neighboring side. You will see the diamond-shaped star points appear. Erase any unnecessary lines to make the 3 pattern shapes (diamond, square, and triangle) easier to see.

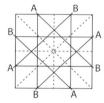
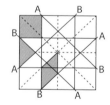

Once you've become comfortable with using a compass and have mastered drafting the simple Eight-Pointed Star, you may wish to experiment with other, octagon-based blocks, such as Kaleidoscope and Castle Wall.

The Kaleidoscope and Castle Wall blocks are also based on the octagon shape.

DRAFTING A HEXAGON (HEXIE)

A hexagon—popularly called a "hexie"—is a six-sided shape with all sides equal. Grandmother's Flower Garden is probably the most commonly recognized of all hexie-based quilt block patterns.

The basic hexie shape

Quilt in progress—some pieced hexies

Drafting a hexagon begins with a circle, which means you'll be working with the compass again. Nothing to it—by now you're an expert!

When Hexie Size Doesn't Matter

Often, when planning a single-patch quilt, you can draft a hexagon to any random size, make a template (see When You Need Templates, page 47), and begin cutting. So let's use a randomly sized hexie as an example. Once you're comfortable with the easy mechanics involved, I'll show you how to draft a hexie to any specific size you wish.

1. Open your compass to any random measurement (2″ is a good size for experimentation). This measurement will equal the *radius* of your circle and won't be changed throughout the drafting process. Hold your compass steady and draw a circle.

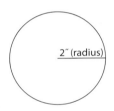

2. Without changing the measurement, place the point of your compass at any random place on the circle. Swing the compass to the left to make a pencil mark that cuts the circle's perimeter.

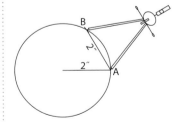

3. Repeat Step 2, but this time using the mark that you've just made on the circumference (or perimeter) of the circle as your starting point for the next mark. Work your way around the entire circumference of the circle until you've made 6 equidistant marks.

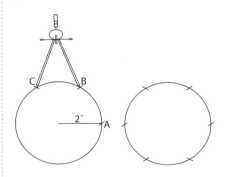

4. Use your ruler to connect the marks at the exact point at which they break the circle. There's your hexie!

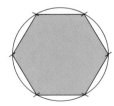

When Hexie Size *Does* Matter

There may be occasions when you want your hexagon to finish to a specific size—say 1½"
along its side or 5" at its widest point. How do you do that? No problem!

To draft a hexagon with a specific side measurement:
The radius of the circle you draw will be the same as the side measurement of the finished hexie. If you want a hexie that measures 1½" on its side, begin by opening your compass to draw a circle with a 1½" radius.

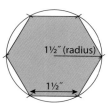

Drafting a hexie to a specific side measurement

To draft a hexie of a specific width: The widest point of the finished hexie will be equal to the radius × 2. If you need a hexie that measures 5" across its widest point, begin the drafting process by opening your compass to draw a circle with a radius half that measurement—in this case, 2½".

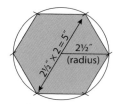

Drafting a hexie to a specific width

Subdividing the Hexie

Once you can draft a hexagon, it's super easy to draft a 60° diamond (think Tumbling Blocks) and a 60° triangle (all sides equal).

The 60° diamond used for Tumbling Blocks is derived from the hexagon.

Draft a hexie of random size (When Hexie Size Doesn't Matter, page 34) or desired size (see When Hexie Size *Does* Matter, above). Use your ruler to divide the shape with a big X across two of the hexie's widest points. The 60° diamond will appear as shown.

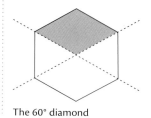

The 60° diamond

Bonus: The "leftover" shape is a 60° triangle!

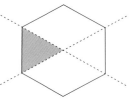

The 60° triangle

■ HITTING THE HIGH POINTS

- ■ *Choose quality, accurate drafting materials.*
- ■ *Work in good light in a comfortable setting.*
- ■ *Examine your chosen block carefully for a potential grid. Is it a four-patch? A nine-patch? A sixteen-patch? Or is it octagon or hexie based?*
- ■ *Choose a finished-sized block that makes for simple math.*
- ■ *Relax, have fun, and enjoy the freedom and the possibilities that your new skills have given you!*

We'll cover making templates in The Ins and Outs of Piecing (page 47).

REV UP YOUR ROTARY CUTTER

If I could only take five quilting items to a desert island, I assure you that my rotary-cutting tools would be on that list, along with my fabric and sewing machine. I consider them absolutely indispensible!

SAFETY FIRST

The rotary cutter is a marvelous invention. It revolutionized the quiltmaking process when it first appeared on the scene back in the late 1970s. It is, however, extremely sharp and, with improper use, potentially dangerous. Before we get into technique, let's take a moment to review a few very important safety tips.

Always close or retract the blade after every cut and before storing your cutter.

Always wear closed-toe shoes while cutting. A dropped cutter can do serious damage to unprotected toes.

Always cut away from yourself.

Always keep your cutter out of reach of inquisitive little hands (and husbands wrapping gifts!).

CARE AND STORAGE OF ROTARY EQUIPMENT

- *To avoid dulling or otherwise damaging the blade, make sure that the mat is free of pins and other obstacles before cutting.*
- *Periodically clean the blade to remove lint buildup between the blade and its cover. Replace the blade with the appropriate (same brand) substitute when it becomes nicked or dull. The packaging should guide you in these important maintenance tasks.*
- *Most rotary rulers feature a hole for hanging. If you can't hang yours, store it in a safe place to avoid cracking or breaking it.*
- *Clean your ruler(s) occasionally with warm soapy water, window cleaner, or rubbing alcohol. Don't use nail polish remover; it will remove the markings.*
- *To avoid warping, always store your rotary mat flat and out of direct sunlight. Never leave it in a hot car.*
- *Wash your mat periodically with warm soapy water or window cleaner.*

BASIC ROTARY-CUTTING TECHNIQUE

Take the time to practice on scrap fabric to familiarize yourself with proper rotary-cutting technique before beginning to cut fabric for your quilt. Start by practicing how to hold the cutter correctly.

Hold the rotary cutter in the hand you write with. Place the handle in your palm and wrap your fingers around the cutter handle. Place your index finger on the dip in the handle and lift your elbow slightly.

Proper position for lefties

Proper position for righties

Hold the cutter at a 90° angle with the blade of the cutter straight up and down, flush against the edge of the ruler. Cut across the fabric, from the hip and away from your body, with a single, smooth motion.

SQUARING UP THE FABRIC

It's important that the fabric be smooth and flat, with the folded edges parallel, before you begin cutting. This ensures that your cut strips will be straight, not angled or wobbly, when you unfold them. Even if you've pressed your fabrics before placing them on the shelf, press them again before cutting into them.

1. Fold the fabric selvage to selvage. Fold the fabric again, lining up the first fold with the selvage, so that you'll be cutting through 4 layers.

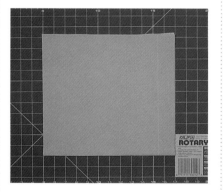

2. Position the fabric on the mat, keeping the folded edges of the fabric aligned with the mat's horizontal lines. Do not let the fabric hang off the table's edge.

tip

It's always a good idea to trim off the selvage edges before sewing into your quilt. These woven edges can cause distortion in sewn seams and are difficult to hand quilt.

3. Line up the vertical lines and horizontal markings on your ruler on or parallel to the grid on the mat. Place the ruler about ½" over the raw edge of the fabric so that the mat, ruler, and fabric are aligned on or parallel to the grids on both the ruler and the mat.

4. Expose the blade on the cutter. Place the blade right next to the ruler along the bottom fold of the fabric. Make a single, smooth pass away from yourself through the fabric to remove the uneven raw or selvage edge.

Cleaning up the fabric edges—lefties

Cleaning up the fabric edges—righties

■ **TROUBLESHOOTING: CUTTING GLITCHES**

If you're having difficulty getting a nice, smooth cut, it may be that:

- ■ *The cutter's blade has become nicked or dull and needs replacement.*
- ■ *You're not exerting enough pressure on the cutter.*
- ■ *You're trying to cut through too many layers for the size cutter you're using (see Rotary Cutter, page 16).*
- ■ *The tension on the blade is either too tight or too loose on the blade assembly.*
- ■ *You're not positioning the blade straight up and down, flush against the ruler.*

One final note: if you are not going to cut the bottom edge of your fabric, extend the ruler slightly past the edge of the fabric and begin your cut on the mat.

CUTTING STRIPS

A strip is the most basic unit used in rotary cutting. Most of the other shapes you'll cut begin with a strip. Use your ruler, not the grid lines on the mat, to establish the correct measurements. *Exception:* If you need to cut a strip of fabric wider than your ruler, use the grid lines on your rotary mat to help you cut this wider strip— or hold or tape two rulers together to make a wider ruler.

Finished width + ½" | Grain

1. Square up the fabric (page 37). Move the ruler over so that it measures the desired finished width of the strip + ½". Line up the vertical measurement on the ruler with the trimmed edge of the fabric, making sure that the fabric and ruler are also aligned with the grid on the cutting mat.

2. Cut a strip as described in Squaring Up the Fabric, Step 4 (at left).

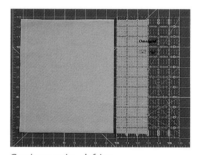
Cutting a strip—lefties

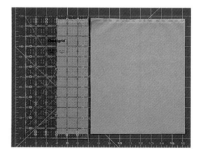
Cutting a strip—righties

Check occasionally that the raw edge of the fabric is still straight; if not, resquare before continuing.

MAGIC NUMBERS

Good news! Each of the following shapes has a "magic" number (or numbers) that you can use to determine the cut size of that particular shape. Because of the angles involved, different shapes have different numbers. The instructions for each shape include a diagram indicating that shape's unique Magic Number(s). See the guide summarizing all the Magic Numbers (below). As you become more familiar with rotary cutting, these numbers will become second nature.

MAGIC NUMBERS: QUICK REFERENCE GUIDE

Here are two basic rules for using Magic Numbers:

- Magic Numbers only work with ¼˝ seam allowances.

- Measure the finished size of the desired shape and then add the Magic Number. This new measurement includes the necessary ¼˝ seam allowances.

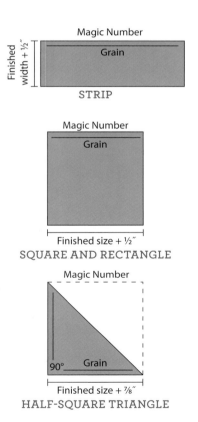

Magic Number

Finished width + ½˝

Grain

STRIP

Magic Number

Grain

Finished size + ½˝

SQUARE AND RECTANGLE

Magic Number

90° Grain

Finished size + ⅞˝

HALF-SQUARE TRIANGLE

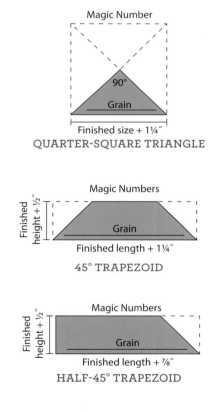

Magic Number

90° Grain

Finished size + 1¼˝

QUARTER-SQUARE TRIANGLE

Magic Numbers

Finished height + ½˝

Grain

Finished length + 1¼˝

45° TRAPEZOID

Magic Numbers

Finished height + ½˝

Grain

Finished length + ⅞˝

HALF-45° TRAPEZOID

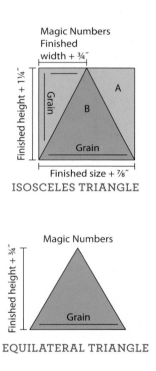

Magic Numbers
Finished width + ¾˝

Finished height + 1¼˝

Grain

A

B

Grain

Finished size + ⅞˝

ISOSCELES TRIANGLE

Magic Numbers

Finished height + ¾˝

Grain

EQUILATERAL TRIANGLE

Magic Numbers

Finished width + ½˝

Grain

Finished size + ½˝

45° DIAMOND

CUTTING SQUARES

Squares are strips subcut into smaller units.

Grain

Finished size + ½"

1. Square up the fabric (page 37) and cut a strip the desired finished size of the square + ½".

2. Reposition the strip horizontally on the cutting mat, on or parallel to one of the mat's horizontal grid lines. Square off the end of the strip to create a clean edge.

3. Move the ruler over so that it measures the desired finished side of the square + ½". (This measurement will be the same as the width of the cut strip.) Cut the square.

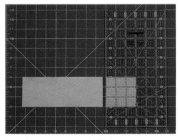

Cutting a square—lefties

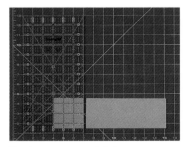

Cutting a square—righties

CUTTING RECTANGLES

Rectangles are strips subcut into smaller units.

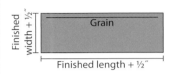

Finished width + ½"

Grain

Finished length + ½"

1. Square up the fabric (page 37) and cut a strip the desired finished height of the rectangle + ½".

2. Reposition the strip horizontally on the cutting mat, on or parallel to one of the mat's horizontal grid lines. Square off the end of the strip to create a clean edge.

3. Move the ruler over so that it measures the desired finished width of the rectangle + ½". Cut the rectangle.

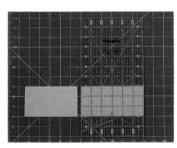

Cutting a rectangle—lefties

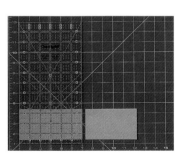

Cutting a rectangle—righties

CUTTING HALF- AND QUARTER- SQUARE TRIANGLES

Both half- and quarter-square triangles are cut from squares. Although they look the same, the difference between the two is the position of the 90° corner to the straight-grain edge(s). This is important, because—whenever possible—you'll want the outside edge of the finished block or unit to fall on the straight of grain (see Fabric Grain, page 18).

The half-square triangle has two sides adjacent to the 90° corner on the straight of grain. The quarter-square triangle has the side opposite the 90° corner on the straight of grain.

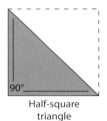

Half-square triangle

Quarter-square triangle

Half-Square Triangles

Each cut square yields two half-square triangles.

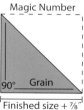

Magic Number

90° Grain

Finished size + ⅞"

1. Square up the fabric (page 37) and cut a strip the desired finished size of the square + ⅞".

2. Reposition the strip horizontally on the cutting mat, on or parallel to one of the mat's horizontal grid lines. Square off the end of the strip to create a clean edge.

3. Move the ruler over so that it measures the desired finished size of the square + ⅞". (This measurement will be the same as the width of the cut strip.) Cut a square.

4. Position the ruler corner to corner and cut the square in half diagonally.

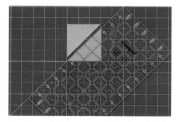

Cutting a half-square triangle—lefties

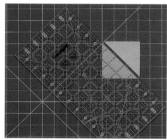

Cutting a half-square triangle—righties

Quarter-Square Triangles

Each cut square yields two quarter-square triangles.

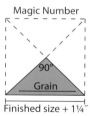

Magic Number

90° Grain

Finished size + 1¼"

1. Square up the fabric (page 37) and cut a strip the desired finished size of the square + 1¼".

2. Reposition the strip horizontally on the cutting mat, on or parallel to one of the mat's horizontal grid lines. Square off the end of the strip to create a clean edge.

3. Move the ruler over so that it measures the desired finished size of the square + 1¼". (This measurement will be the same as the width of the cut strip.) Cut the square.

4. Position the ruler corner to corner and cut the square in half diagonally.

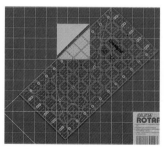

Cutting a quarter-square triangle, first cut—lefties

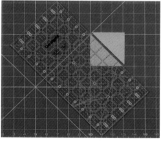

Cutting a quarter-square triangle, first cut—righties

5. Cut the square in half again, on the opposite diagonal.

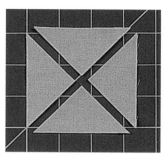

Cutting a quarter-square triangle, second cut—lefties

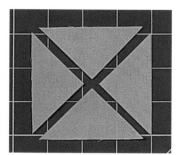

Cutting a quarter-square triangle, second cut—righties

CUTTING 45° TRAPEZOIDS

A 45° trapezoid is a rectangle with each end cut on a 45° angle in opposite directions. To achieve this shape, you'll use the 45° marking on your ruler.

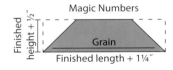

Magic Numbers

Finished height + ½″ | Grain | Finished length + 1¼″

1. Square up the fabric (page 37) and cut a strip the desired finished height of the trapezoid + ½″.

2. Reposition the strip horizontally on the cutting mat, on or parallel to one of the mat's horizontal grid lines. Square off the end of the strip to create a clean edge.

3. Cut a rectangle the desired finished length of the trapezoid + 1¼″.

4. Align the 45° angle on your ruler with the horizontal edge of the rectangle as shown. Carefully cut the end of the strip from the bottom corner to the top edge.

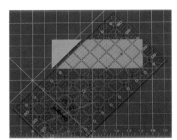

Cutting the first 45° angle—
lefties

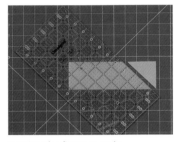

Cutting the first 45° angle—
righties

5. Turn the shape top to bottom (180°) by rotating either the mat or the shape itself. Align the 45° angle on your ruler with the edge of the shape as shown and cut.

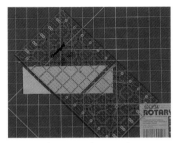

Cutting the second 45° angle—
lefties

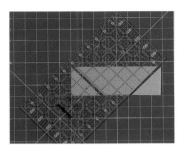

Cutting the second 45° angle—
righties

CUTTING AN ISOSCELES TRIANGLE IN A SQUARE

Cutting an isosceles triangle in a square involves cutting two shapes: the background triangles (A), which are mirror images of each other, and the isosceles triangle itself (B). Note that the *sides* of the isosceles triangle are of a different measurement than the *base* of the triangle.

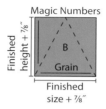

Magic Numbers

Background Triangles (A)

The background of an isosceles triangle in a square has two sides: a left- and a right-facing side (mirror images). You must cut the background in double layers, with like sides together. This will give you the correct, mirror-imaged shapes.

1. Square up the fabric (page 37) and cut a strip the desired finished short side of the triangle + ¾".

2. Reposition the strip horizontally, on or parallel to one of the grid lines on the mat. Square off the end of the strip to create a clean edge.

3. Open and refold the strip so that there are 2 layers of fabric, with *like sides together*. Cut once to yield 2 rectangles the finished length of the triangle + 1¼".

4. Keeping the rectangles stacked, cut the rectangles in half diagonally in one direction to create 2 each of the left- and right-facing background rectangles.

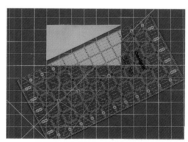

Cutting the background triangles—lefties

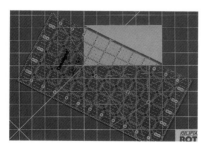

Cutting the background triangles—righties

Isosceles Triangles (B)

It's easy to cut individual isosceles triangles.

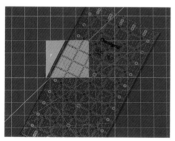

Magic Numbers

1. Square up the fabric (page 37) and cut a strip the desired finished size of the base of the triangle + ⅞".

2. Reposition the strip horizontally, on or parallel to one of the grid lines on the mat. Square off the end of the strip.

3. Cut a square the finished size of the triangle + ⅞".

4. Fold the square in half to find the top center and cut from the bottom corner to the top center.

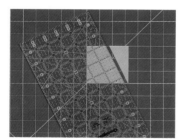

Cutting the first side of the triangle—lefties

Cutting the first side of the triangle—righties

5. Rotate the mat or the shape, and cut from the (now) bottom center to the upper corner.

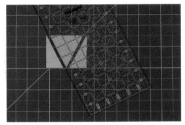

Cutting the opposite side of the triangle—lefties

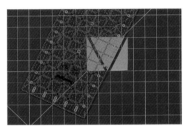

Cutting the opposite side of the triangle—righties

note

If all your isosceles triangles will be cut from the same fabric, cut a strip the desired finished height of the triangle + ⅞″. Measure and mark the desired finished base of the triangle + ⅞″. Fold the base in half to find the top point and then cut as shown.

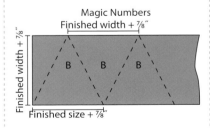

Magic Numbers
Finished width + ⅞″

Finished width + ⅞″

B   B   B

Finished size + ⅞″

CUTTING EQUILATERAL TRIANGLES

All three sides of an equilateral triangle are equal in length. This triangle starts with a strip. To achieve this shape, you will use the 60° marking on your ruler. When working with equilateral triangles, measure the distance between the top and the base of the triangle (the height) and add ¾″.

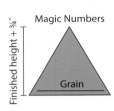

Magic Numbers

Finished height + ¾″

Grain

1. Square up the fabric (page 37) and cut a strip the desired finished height of the triangle + ¾″.

2. Reposition the strip horizontally, on or parallel to one of the grid lines on the mat. Square off the end of the strip.

3. Align the 60° marking on the ruler with the bottom edge of the strip as shown; cut.

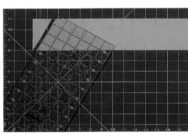

Cutting the first 60° angle— lefties

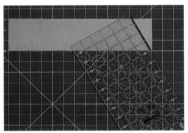

Cutting the first 60° angle— righties

4. Rotate the ruler so that the other 60° marking is aligned with the top edge of the strip; cut.

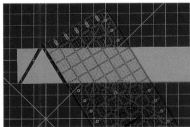

Cutting the second 60° angle— lefties

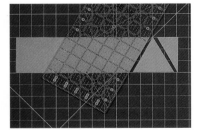

Cutting the second 60° angle— righties

Before cutting additional triangles, verify that the measurement of the triangle from top to bottom is the measurement of the initial cut strip (see Step 1). If your 60° cut is off, the error will show up here.

CUTTING 45° DIAMONDS

Diamonds also start with a strip. Measure the distance between the two sets of parallel sides and add ½" to each measurement. To achieve this shape, you will use the 45° marking on your ruler.

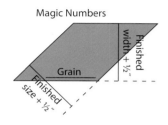

Magic Numbers

1. Square up the fabric (page 37) and cut a strip the desired finished width of the diamond + ½".

2. Reposition the strip horizontally, on or parallel to one of the grid lines on the mat. Square off the end of the strip.

3. Align the 45° marking on the ruler with the top horizontal edge of the strip as shown; cut.

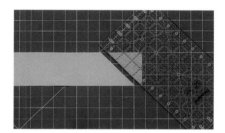

Cutting the first 45° angle—lefties

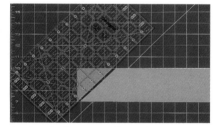

Cutting the first 45° angle—righties

4. Slide your ruler across the strip to the appropriate measurement, keeping the 45° marking aligned with the edge of the strip. (Remember: you are measuring the width between the parallel sides.) Make the second 45° cut.

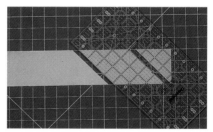

Cutting the second 45° angle—lefties

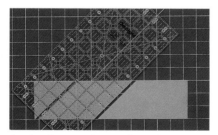

Cutting the second 45° angle—righties

note

If the diamond is elongated, the pieced unit will have a left and right side (mirror image). Cut a strip the finished width + ½" across the full width of the fabric. Open and refold the strip so that there are two layers of fabric, with *like sides together*, carefully aligning the edges. Cut at a 45° angle. Move the ruler to make the appropriate second 45° cut.

■ DETERMINING WHAT A STRIP WILL YIELD

Although fabric typically measures approximately 42″ wide on the bolt, it's a good idea to base your calculations on fabric (and subsequently strips) that measures 40″ wide from selvage to selvage. This allows for potential shrinkage that might occur when the fabric is laundered and from any width lost with the removal of selvages.

Here's an easy method for determining how many shapes of the desired size a cut strip will yield. For our example, let's use a 2½″ × 4½″ rectangle.

1. Cut a strip that equals the height of the desired shape; in this case, 2½″.

2. Divide 40″ by the length of the shape; for a 2½″ × 4½″ rectangle, you'll be dividing 40″ by 4½″. The result is 8.8, which means that you can cut 8 complete 2½″ × 4½″ rectangles from a 2½″ × 40″ strip.

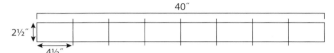

A 2½″ × 40″ strip yields 8 complete rectangles, each 2½″ × 4½″.

Once you know this number, it's easy to figure how many strips you'll need to cut (and how much yardage you'll need to purchase) to yield the required number of rectangles.

Let's say your quilt calls for 96 rectangles, each 2½″ × 4½″.

1. Divide the total number of rectangles needed by the number of rectangles you can cut from a strip. In the case of our example, that would be 96 ÷ 8 = 12. Therefore, you'll need 12 strips, each 2½″ wide, to yield the required 96 rectangles.

2. Multiply the number of strips × the strip width; in this case, 12 strips × 2½″ = 30″. Since it's always a good idea to round up a bit to allow for shrinkage, straightening edges, and potential goofs, I would purchase 36″, or 1 yard, of fabric for 96 rectangles.

CUTTING BIAS STRIPS

Unlike strips cut on the straight grain (crosswise or lengthwise), strips cut on the bias of the fabric (see Fabric Grain, page 18) stretch nicely, making them ideal for curved appliqués such as vines and stems (see Preparing Vines and Stems, page 76) or for making bias bindings (see Straight-Grain vs. Bias Binding, page 156).

1. Square up the fabric (page 37).

2. Place the fabric on your cutting mat, aligning the straightened edge of the fabric with a vertical line on the mat. Position your ruler so that the 45° marking is aligned with the straight edge of the fabric.

3. Cut across the fabric. Move the ruler over so that it measures the desired cut width of the strip, aligning the long edge of the ruler with the trimmed 45° fabric edge.

4. Cut the strip.

5. Repeat Steps 3 and 4 until you have the number of strips required for your quilt.

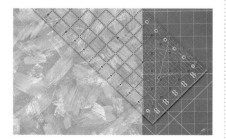

Position the ruler.

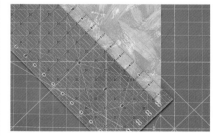

Position the ruler.

Position the ruler and cut.

THE INS AND OUTS OF PIECING

WHAT YOU'LL NEED

- Sharp (or mechanical) pencil
- Pencil sharpener (*optional*)
- Eraser
- Template material
- Scissors: paper
- Ruler: Thin 2˝ × 18˝ acrylic, gridded, see-through ruler
- Masking tape

WHEN YOU NEED TEMPLATES

While rotary cutting is a wonderful invention and Magic Numbers (page 39) make cutting properly sized fabric shapes a breeze, there may come a time when only a pattern piece will do.

Patterns designed for machine piecing typically include a ¼˝ seam allowance on all sides. An exactly cut, consistent ¼˝ seam allowance enables you to match the raw edges of your fabric shapes accurately and effortlessly.

Happily, this seam allowance is usually already included in patterns that appear in print, such as in books and magazines. Just tape a piece of sturdy template material over each pattern piece, use a sharp (or mechanical) pencil and ruler to trace the shapes, and cut directly on the marked lines. Transfer any information from the printed pattern pieces—for example, block name, identifying letters, and grainline arrows—onto your templates, and you're good to go.

Adding a Seam Allowance to Drafted Patterns

If you're working with a block you've drafted yourself, you'll need to add seam allowances before tracing the patterns to make templates. Squares and rectangles are pretty straightforward.

Triangles and other shapes with angles greater or less than 90° can be a bit trickier. Take advantage of the grid on the graph paper whenever possible to add ¼″ to the edges of the shape. Use the ¼″ marking on your gridded see-through ruler to add ¼″ to the remaining edge(s).

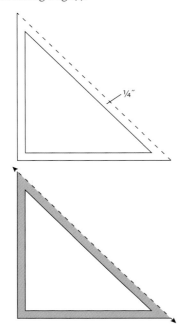

Once you've added the ¼″ seam allowances, tape a piece of sturdy template material over each pattern piece, use a sharp (or mechanical) pencil and ruler to trace the shapes (with the newly added seam allowances), and cut directly on the marked lines. Finish by adding the block name, identifying letters, and grainline arrows to each template.

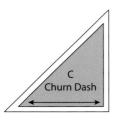

MACHINE PIECING

Once the fabrics are chosen and the pieces cut, it's time to sit down at your sewing machine and start stitching.

WHAT YOU'LL NEED

- Sewing machine
- Pins
- Scissors
- Stiletto
- Seam ripper
- Iron and pressing station (firm surface)
- Masking tape (*optional*)

Pinning

When it comes to pinning, you'll meet those who pin and those who don't. I've found that the little time it takes to pin can determine the success of the block and ultimately the quilt. Basically, you should pin where there are seams and intersections that need to line up. Here are a few guidelines.

- When aligning seams that are pressed in opposite directions (see Pressing Matters, page 52), place a pin in both sides of the seam, no more than ⅛″ from the seamline, and directly where the ¼″ seam will be sewn.

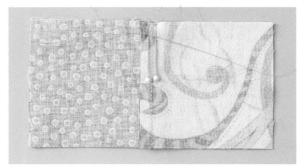

Pin seams pressed in opposite directions.

■ If points need to be matched exactly (as in the center of a Pinwheel block):

A. *With right sides together, place the first pin in the wrong side of one unit, exactly at the intersection of the seams. Carefully open the units to make sure the pin is also piercing the point exactly in the right side of the second unit. Adjust if necessary. Reclose the units and press the head of the pin firmly through both layers.*

Insert the first pin at the intersection.

B. *While holding the first pin firmly in place, place the second and third pin on each side of the intersection, no more than ⅛" from the first pin.*

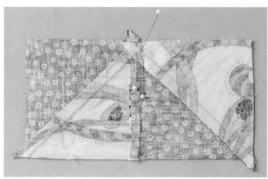

Insert the second and third pins.

C. *Just before placing the unit under your sewing machine's presser foot, loosen the first pin, allowing it to dangle loosely. Stitch with the pinned piece on top. As you approach the intersection, remove the first pin at the last second and let the sewing machine needle drop into that hole. If your sewing machine doesn't sew over pins easily, remove the second and third pins right before you stitch over them.*

Aligning Differently Shaped Pieces

Sometimes you'll be called upon to join shapes that do not appear to fit together. If your cutting has been handled correctly, it's just a question of learning how the shapes fit. Here are some common examples.

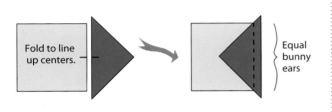

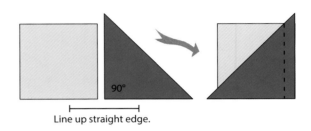

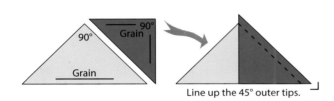

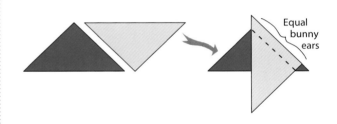

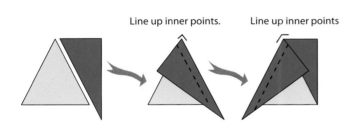

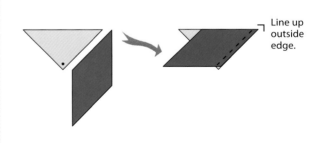

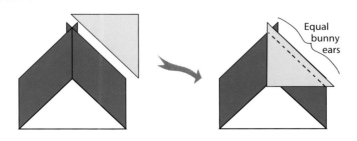

Stitching

Set the stitch length on your machine just long enough so that your seam ripper slides nicely in under the stitches. Backstitching usually isn't necessary, because you'll cross all the seam ends with other seams.

The All-Important ¼" Seam Allowance

An accurate ¼" seam is key to precise piecing. "Close enough" will only reward you with yards of frustration. If your block units, finished blocks, and other pieced elements are not coming out to the correct size or are sized inconsistently, it may be time to check that you are sewing a perfect, consistent ¼" seam. Here's a little trick I learned from "piecer *par excellance*" Sally Collins. Cut two strips of fabric, each measuring 1" × 3½". Sew the two strips together along a 3½" side, press, and then measure. The sewn unit should be *exactly* 1½" wide. If not, try again until you find your machine's perfect ¼".

1 ½"

If you continue to have difficulty achieving accurate results, your problem might be the thickness of your thread. You may find that sewing *just a hair* inside the typical ¼" does the trick.

Another issue that can affect your accuracy is the tendency to "wander off" at the end of a line of stitching, resulting in a less-than-exact and wobbly seam. Use a stiletto (see Stiletto and Seam Ripper, page 17) to hold in place the end of the unit you are sewing for a clean, accurate result.

Inaccurate piecing—stitching trails off

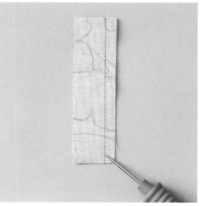

Accurate piecing—straight, consistent ¼" seam

Some sewing machines come with a foot (or attachment) that measures an exact ¼". If your machine doesn't have this feature, you can mark the throat plate to compensate. Place your clear plastic rotary ruler under the sewing-machine needle and drop the presser foot; then manually ease the needle down on top of the ¼" mark. Use a narrow piece of colored tape to carefully mark the ¼" spot on the throat plate, using the edge of the ruler as your guide. (For additional insurance, some quilters use both the ¼" foot and the tape.)

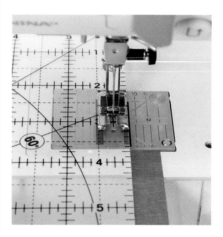

tip

If the units you're stitching are not exactly the same size and you've eased the difference with pins, sew with the layer that needs to be eased on the bottom, against the throat plate. The action of the feed dogs will gently assist the easing process.

Pressing Matters

Pressing is a very important part of the quiltmaking process. Many quilters approach pressing as though they were ironing the weekly laundry. Not a good idea. The desired technique it to lift and place the iron in an up-and-down motion, rather than to drag it from side to side across the surface of the fabric, stretching and distorting as you go. This is especially important for exposed bias edges, as they are easily distorted. In fact, I avoid pressing exposed bias edges … period.

For piecing, press on a firm surface, such as an ironing board with a single pad. It's customary to press seams to one side or the other, toward the darker fabric if possible, though occasionally you'll make an exception if it suits the piecing sequence.

Begin by pressing the seam to set the stitches. Then flip open the sewn pieces and press from the wrong side. Finish by pressing from the right side of the unit, block, or quilt top. This prevents tucks being pressed into the sewn seams.

▣ TO STEAM OR NOT TO STEAM

Personally, as I'm so careful when I press and so cautious about avoiding exposed bias edges, I have no problem pressing with steam. You are probably the best judge of whether this is a viable practice for you.

Regardless, steam can come in handy when the block is completely assembled. Typically, all outside edges of the block will fall on the straight grain (no exposed bias), and a careful steam press helps produce a nice, crisp, flat outcome.

"Unsewing" (a.k.a. Seam Ripping)

Once in awhile, you'll need to "unsew" (that is, pick out) a seam. Not fun, but occasionally necessary. Here's how you do it: use your seam ripper to cut every third stitch on one side of the seam, and then lift the thread off the other side.

If you need to pick out a seam that joins bias edges, as in a Flying Geese unit (see Sew-and-Flip Method, Step 5, page 55), consider tossing the unit and starting over. It's highly likely that the bias edges will stretch and won't fit properly when you attempt to restitch them.

MACHINE-PIECING TECHNIQUES YOU'LL WANT TO KNOW

A number of wonderful, accurate, and time-saving techniques can greatly improve your machine-piecing experience.

Strip Piecing

With this versatile technique, strips of fabric are sewn together along their long edges to make strip sets. Once they're pressed, these strip sets (sometimes called *strata*) are subcut into "slices" that can be arranged to form any number of units and blocks.

1. Aligning the long raw edges, place 2 strips of the desired width, right sides together; pin if you like.

2. Stitch along the long raw edge with a ¼" seam. Press (usually toward the darker strip).

3. Cut the strip set into slices of the desired finished width, plus ½″ for seam allowance. The slices can be arranged and sewn to make four-patch units, pieced borders, and so on.

4. You can sew more than two strips together to make a strip set. The results have all kinds of possibilities for use in blocks and borders.

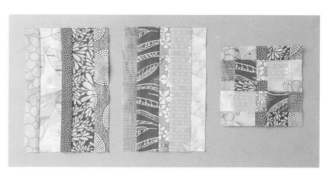

Nine-Patch Variation Quilt
(30½″ × 30½″) pieced and machine
quilted by Pam Vieira-McGinnis

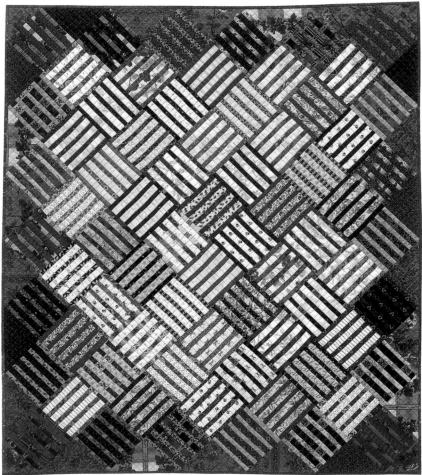

Rail Fence (47" × 55") designed and made by Alex Anderson, machine quilted by Paula Reid

Sew-and-Flip Method

You can use this easy and efficient technique when you need to sew a half-square triangle to a single larger shape to yield a unit that finishes as a rectangle or a larger square—for example, to make a flying geese or square-in-a-square unit. You'll love it: you won't need to cut or sew a raw bias edge, minimizing the potential for stretching and distortion.

▣ MAGIC NUMBERS

Cut the squares (A) equal to the finished short side of the unit plus ½". When pinned, sewn, and trimmed, these squares form the half-square triangles in the finished unit.

Cut the rectangle or other shape to which the squares will be sewn (B) equal to the finished size of the unit plus ½" in both directions.

Finished unit

Finished short side of unit + ½"

Finished short side of unit + ½"

Finished long side of unit + ½"

For our example, let's use a 2″ × 4″ finished flying geese unit.

1. Cut 2 squares 2½″ × 2½″ for A and 1 rectangle 2½″ × 4½″ from a different fabric for B.

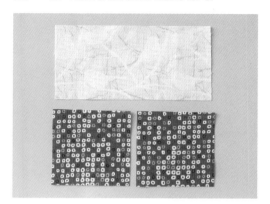

2. Draw a line diagonally in one direction of the wrong side of each A square. With right sides together, align a marked square with one end of the B rectangle.

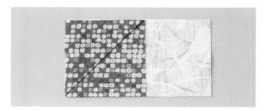

3. Sew directly on the drawn line and trim, leaving a ¼″ seam allowance.

4. Press toward the corner.

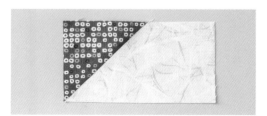

5. Repeat Steps 2–4 to mark and sew an A square to the opposite end of the B piece.

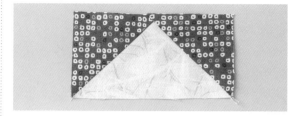

Once you're familiar with this technique, you'll find dozens of ways to use it.

tip

If your A squares are cut from a directional fabric (see Feathers and Paisleys and Stripes, page 23, and Examples of Directional Fabric, page 105), place the A squares so the direction of the print runs *opposite* to the direction you wish it to appear in the final unit or block.

Secret Star-Point Method

You'll love this easy and efficient method for making star-point units *four at a time*. (Some quilters refer to this technique as Four-in-One Flying Geese.)

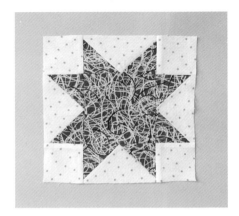

■ MAGIC NUMBERS FOR SECRET STAR-POINT METHOD

Cut the small squares (A) equal to the finished short side of the unit plus ⅞″. When pinned, sewn, and trimmed, these squares form the half-square triangles in the finished unit.

Cut the large square (B) equal to the finished long side of the unit plus 1¼″.

Finished unit

Magic Number =
Finished short side
of unit + ⅞″

Magic Number =
Finished long side of unit + 1¼″

Once again, let's use a 2″ × 4″ finished unit.

1. Cut 4 squares 2⅞″ × 2⅞″ for A and 1 square 5¼″ × 5¼″ from a different fabric for B.

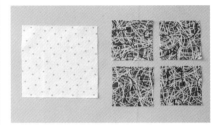

2. Draw a diagonal line on the wrong side of each of the 4 smaller (A) squares. This will be your cutting line. Draw a second set of lines ¼″ from the original diagonal line on both sides. These will be your sewing lines.

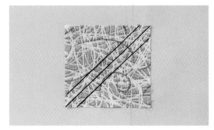

Draw diagonal lines.

3. Place 2 marked squares, right sides together, on opposite corners of the larger square as shown. Stitch carefully on the 2 outer lines.

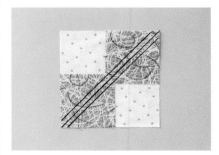

Stitch on the outermost lines.

4. Cut on the marked line between the lines of stitching; press open, toward the triangles.

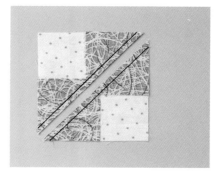

Cut on the unsewn line and press.

5. Place a third marked square, right sides together, with an open corner of the unit from Step 4 as shown. Stitch on the 2 outer lines. Cut on the line between the lines of stitching. Repeat this step, using the last marked square and the remaining unit from Step 4.

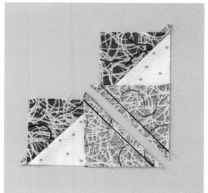

Stitch and cut on the unsewn line.

6. Press each unit. You now have 4 finished units!

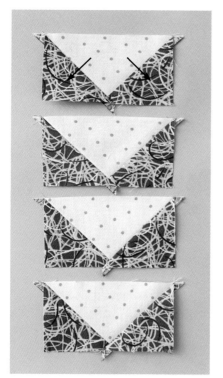

Press.

Y-Seams

Many blocks, like the grid-based blocks described in Drafting Blocks Based on Grids (page 32), are pieced in vertical, horizontal, or diagonal rows. Sometimes, however, the piecing sequence for a block requires you to take a little detour in the seam so that you can insert a neighboring piece. This is called an inset or Y-seam. The star points of an Eight-Pointed Star (see Drafting an Eight-Pointed Star, page 33) are good examples.

On the wrong side, mark a dot ¼″ from the corner side edges of the piece(s) that will be inset. This is the stop-and-start point you'll use to create the Y-seam.

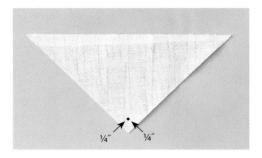

Follow the diagram below for the piecing sequence. The numbers indicate the order in which to sew the seams, and the arrows indicate the direction to sew. Always backstitch at the dot where the seams meet. Use a neutral-colored thread or a thread to match the star diamonds so that your stitches remain invisible.

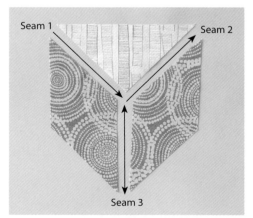

Seam 3 can be sewn in either direction.

Press the center seam (between diamonds) open first, then press side seams away from the set-in triangle.

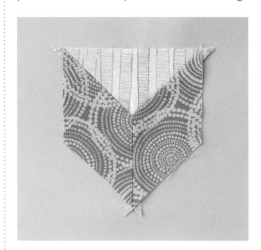

Sewing Curves

Sewing curves is easy! Just take your time on the first few blocks until you get the hang of things. You'll be breezing through your Drunkard's Path, Fan, and other curved blocks in no time!

Some quilters sew with the background piece down and the "belly" piece facing them. Some quilters—myself included—prefer to sew with the "belly" side down and the background piece facing up. You might want to experiment with pinning and piecing both ways to see which option is more comfortable for you.

1. Trace pattern pieces ("belly" and "background") onto a piece of sturdy template material. Be sure to transfer the tick marks along the curved edges on both pieces.

2. Use the templates to carefully trace the shapes onto the wrong wide of the desired fabrics. Transfer the tick marks from the templates to the fabric pieces.

3. Cut out the fabric pieces directly on the traced lines.

4. Carefully make a few clips in the curved edge of the background piece, taking care not to clip beyond the ¼" seam allowance.

5. With right sides together, pin the background to the belly. Match the midpoints first, then the ends, and then the in-between tick marks, adding extra pins if you wish. Because the curves are cut on the bias, you can manipulate the pieces to follow the curves. The clips you made in Step 4 will help you here also.

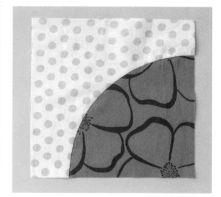

6. Sew the pieces together along the pinned curved edges, taking care to stitch an accurate ¼"; remove the pins as you go.

7. Pressing from the right side of the block, press the seams toward the background.

Press from the *right side* of the block.

PAPER-FOUNDATION PIECING

Paper-foundation piecing makes it possible to use specialty fabrics that quilters usually avoid: silk, rayon, lamé—the entire range of unruly, stretchy, slippery "rebel" fabrics. However, for your first few paper-piecing projects, I suggest you stick to the 100% cotton fabrics already in your stash. Flannels tend to have a mind of their own but don't slip and move as much as the aforementioned fabric "rebels."

Paper-foundation piecing is also excellent for blocks with exposed bias edges and tiny points, which I had avoided in the past. These are easily made using paper piecing. You can approach difficult patterns with the confidence that they will come out perfectly.

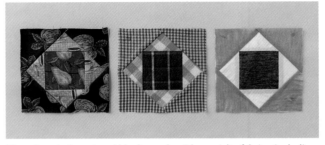

Three foundation-pieced blocks made with specialty fabrics, including silks and flannels

WHAT YOU'LL NEED

- Sewing machine
- Rotary cutter
- Rotary mat
- Rotary ruler

- Paper for foundation patterns. *Options include:*

  - **Vellum** is a high-grade tracing paper used by architects and artists. While Simple Foundations Translucent Vellum (C&T Publishing; see Resources, page 174) is a little more costly, it's worth the price. I strongly recommend this option for beginners. Because it is translucent, it makes lining up the fabric pieces a breeze. Vellum is very easy to remove. You'll need to use a larger needle and a shorter stitch. If you have problems with the photocopy machine jamming, you'll need to use regular 20-weight computer/photocopy paper.

  - **Carol Doak's Foundation Paper** (by C&T Publishing, see Resources, page 174) is easy to remove, the price is right, and it doesn't curl when you iron it.

  - **Computer or photocopy machine paper (20-weight)** works quite nicely for foundation piecing. It's easy to find and reasonably priced. It holds up very well when you have to pick out any sewing mistakes. However, it's difficult to see through when you are arranging the fabric in the correct position, so you'll need access to good light.

  - **Typing paper** is thinner and a little more transparent than computer paper. It's less durable than computer paper but is easier to remove. Again, you'll need to use a shorter stitch length and larger needle. This paper should go through the photocopy machine fine, but if you have problems with the photocopy machine jamming, use regular 20-weight computer/photocopy machine paper.

  - **Examination paper** is very lightweight and is readily available if you have a generous doctor. Examination paper works great with the needle-punch method (see Creating Patterns, page 62). You can use a slightly larger stitch, and it's easy to remove.

Sizing Fabric Pieces

In traditional patchwork, pieces are cut to the exact size and shape, plus a ¼" seam allowance on all sides. When paper-foundation piecing, you'll rough cut pieces slightly larger than necessary. Yes, you'll waste a bit of fabric, but I think you'll agree that what you gain in accuracy and simplicity of piecing is well worth it.

If you're cutting strips, cut each strip at least ½" wider and longer than the area you will cover on the paper foundation.

If you're using half-square triangles, cut the square at least 1" larger than the area you'll cover on the paper foundation, and then cut the square diagonally from corner to corner.

If you're using quarter-square triangles, cut the square at least 1½" larger than the area you will cover on the paper foundation, and then cut the square diagonally from corner to corner in both directions.

After you've sewn each piece to the foundation, you'll trim the seam allowance to the standard ¼".

- **Machine needle:** A universal or sharp needle (80/12 or 90/14). This needle will make slightly larger holes to help the paper tear away for easy removal.

- **Tape:** Sometimes you'll need to pick out seams. Because the stitch length is smaller than usual, this can cause the paper to tear on the sewn line. You can use removable tape sparingly to create a temporary bond to hold the pieces together, but never use a hot iron directly on the tape—the tape will melt. Another option is Sewer's Fix-It Tape (see Resources, page 174), which you can iron over.

- **Small or wand iron:** Along with the full-sized, all-purpose iron you typically use for your quilting projects, you'll find a small or wand iron extremely useful for pressing each sewn seam. It's easy to maneuver, uses much less energy than a traditional iron, and gets plenty hot.

- **Add-A-Quarter Ruler:** These special rulers have a ¼" lip that makes it very easy to trim seam allowances when paper piecing.

- **Surgical tweezers:** These sharp-nosed tweezers are helpful for removing the tiny shreds of paper that can get caught in the seams when most of the paper is torn away.

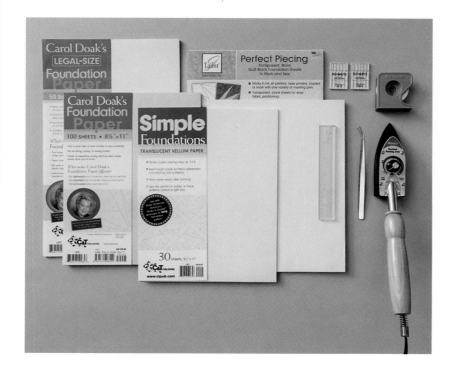

Creating Patterns

Typically, you'll photocopy the paper pattern multiple times. Sometimes distortion can occur during the copy process, so test the accuracy of a sample photocopy by comparing it to the original *before* making multiple copies. Then use the same original and the same copier to make all duplicates.

Another option is to use the needle-punch method to transfer the original pattern to paper. Stack and staple several layers of paper with the pattern on top. Remove the thread from your sewing machine and equip it with an old needle. Sew through all the layers on the drawn lines. After sewing, remove the staples. Not only will the lines be marked, but the paper will also be easier to remove when the unit or block is complete.

You'll note that the only seam allowances on the pattern are on the outer edges of the unit, not on each individual shape. The lines in the interior of the pattern are sewing lines, and the fabric shapes are added in numerical order as indicated on the pattern.

Sewing

Set your sewing machine to sew a smaller-than-usual stitch—for example, 18–20 stitches per inch. The stitches should be tight enough to perforate the paper for easy paper removal but not so tight that seam ripping becomes an impossible task.

1. Cut out the paper pattern just outside the outermost (needle-punched or photocopied) line.

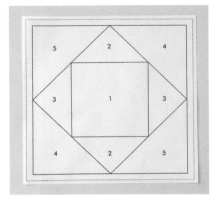

2. Turn the paper pattern face down, unprinted side up.

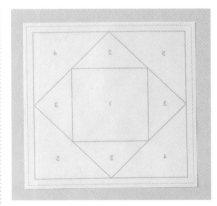

3. Position piece 1 right side up over area 1 on the unprinted side of the pattern, making sure the fabric covers the area completely and extends beyond the area boundaries by a minimum ¼" on all sides. If necessary, hold the pattern to the light so you can see the lines easily.

Position piece 1.

4. Position piece 2 right sides together with piece 1, matching the raw edges along the edge that will be sewn. Pin. Flip piece 2 open and check to make sure it will cover area 2 when sewn, allowing for a ¼" seam allowance on all sides. Adjust if necessary.

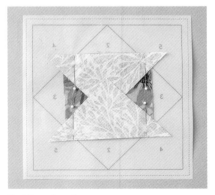

Position piece 2.

5. Turn the paper pattern over to the printed side and stitch *directly on the line* between areas 1 and 2. Finger-press open to verify that the outer edges of piece 2 extend a minimum of ¼" beyond the boundaries of area 2 for seam allowances. Turn the pattern back to the fabric side and press open.

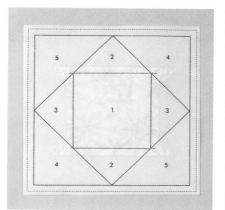

Stitch.

Press.

6. Repeat Steps 4 and 5 to pin and sew piece 3 directly on the line between areas 1 and 3.

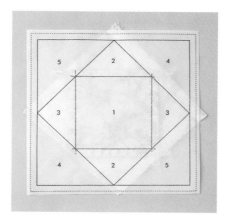

7. Fold the paper pattern back along the line between area 2/3 and area 4 to reveal any excess fabric in the seam allowance. Place a rotary ruler (or Add-A-Quarter Ruler) along the edge of the paper and trim the seam allowance to ¼". Repeat this step for the seam allowances between areas 2/3 and 5.

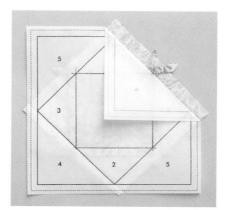

Fold.

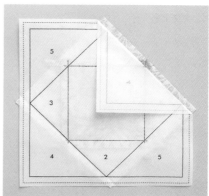

Trim.

8. Open the paper pattern and fold open piece 2 and piece 3. Press with a wand or dry iron.

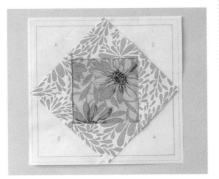

Press.

9. Add the remaining pieces in numerical sequence, trimming and pressing as described in Steps 7 and 8 (page 63 and above), until all the fabric pieces have been sewn to the paper foundation. Press.

10. Turn the unit paper side up. Use your rotary cutter and rotary ruler (or scissors, if the edges of the unit are curved) to trim the excess fabric even with the outermost lines on the paper pattern, creating a ¼" seam allowance on all sides.

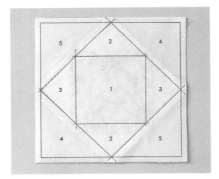

Leave the paper foundation in place for now. (If you remove the papers before the blocks are joined and borders added, you run the risk of distorting exposed bias edges.) When the quilt top is *finished*, use your favorite tools (such as scissors, tweezers, or a seam ripper) to remove all paper foundations.

Sewing Units into Blocks

Sometimes a block is composed of more than one foundation-pieced unit. If so, construct the individual units required and pin the units, fabric sides together, matching the raw edges as usual. Sew the units together with a ¼" seam. (The ¼" sewing line will be visible on the paper pattern to help you sew an accurate seam.)

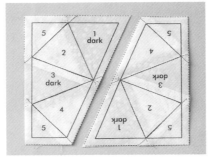

Two halves, paper side up

Two halves, fabric side up

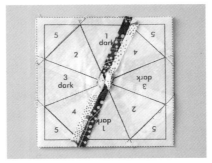

Completed block, paper side up

Completed block, fabric side up

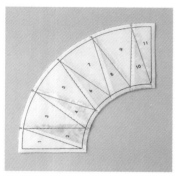

Some blocks call for units that are paper pieced in strips, rather than in blocks. The pointed section (arc) of the New York Beauty block is a good example. The process is basically the same, except that you'll start piecing at one end of the unit and add successive pieces until the unit is complete. Just follow the numbers on the pattern for the piecing sequence and you'll be fine!

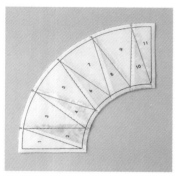

HAND PIECING: ENGLISH PAPER PIECING

While the focus of this chapter is on machine piecing, I couldn't end without including instructions for one very popular hand-piecing technique.

English paper piecing is a hand-piecing technique in which individual shapes are basted over precut paper shapes and then stitched together by hand with tiny stitches in matching or blending thread. It's a great way to join hexies!

WHAT YOU'LL NEED

- Hand needles
- Thread
- Pins
- Scissors
- Rotary cutter
- Rotary mat
- Rotary ruler
- Iron and pressing station
- Heat-resistant template material, sharp (or mechanical) pencil, and paper for individual paper shapes *or* precut paper shapes

Cutting the Shapes

The paper shapes that form the basis for English paper piecing do not include the seam allowance. You'll add the ¼″ seam allowance, either with scissors or rotary cutter, when you cut the fabric pieces.

If you're using purchased, precut paper hexies, you're ready to begin basting, so you can skip to the next section.

If you plan to create papers yourself—for example, if you want them to be a certain size and precut papers aren't available—I recommend that you make a master template from heat-resistant template material and use that to trace the required number of hexie shapes on paper. (You already know how to draft a hexie; see Drafting a Hexagon, page 34.)

Use the paper shapes as a guide for cutting the fabric pieces, making sure to add the seam allowance as you cut.

The AccuQuilt GO! Fabric Cutter system has an optional die set that allows you to cut both the paper templates and the fabric shapes for hexies with 1″ finished sides (see Resources, page 174).

Piecing the Shapes

1. Center a paper shape on the wrong side of a cut fabric shape. Pin the paper to the fabric piece.

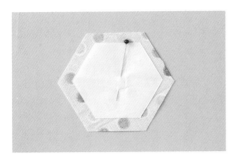

2. Working on one side at a time, fold the seam allowance over the paper. Use a running stitch to baste the seam allowance to the paper shape. You can baste all the shapes at once or do them in batches.

> ### tip
>
> You can also "baste" the seam allowances using a water-soluble Sewline Fabric Glue Pen (see Resources, page 174). When the block has been assembled, press with a steam iron, and the paper templates will "pop" right out.

3. Place 2 basted shapes right sides together. Beginning and ending with a backstitch, sew the shapes together along one side, using small stitches and matching or blending thread. (Some quilters like to use a whipstitch; the goal is to make the stitches as invisible as possible, *whichever* stitch you choose.)

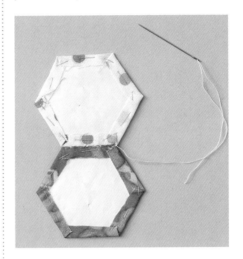

4. When all desired shapes are joined, remove the basting stitches and the paper shapes, and press.

ALL ABOUT APPLIQUÉ

For Hand and Machine Appliqué

- **Pins:** In addition to standard straight pins, some quilters like the tiny sequin pins available at craft stores for appliqué.

- **Scissors**

- **Marking tools**

- **Heat-resistant template material**

- **Lightbox or light table**

- **Stiletto**

- **Iron and pressing station**

- **Mini (wand) iron:** This handy tool (see Small or Wand Iron, page 61) is especially helpful for preparing appliqués with the spray-starch technique. It makes maneuvering those turn-under seam allowances *so much* easier!

- **Freezer paper:** The two different sides of freezer paper—one a dull, paper finish you can write on; the other coated with plastic that sticks to your fabric when pressed with a hot, dry iron—make it perfect to use for appliqué templates. You can purchase freezer paper by the roll at your local grocery store.

- **Lightweight iron-on fusible web:** Fusible web is a heat-activated, synthetic fiber that, when placed between two pieces of fabric and pressed, bonds the layers together. You can purchase fusible web in packaged sheets or off the bolt. Many brands are available; my personal favorite is Appli-kay Wonder Pressure Sensitive Fusible by Floriani (see Resources, page 174). It is lightweight, is incredibly soft, adheres but can be repositioned until pressed for a permanent bond, and is easy to stitch through. Whichever brand of fusible you select, make sure to read the manufacturer's directions for use (usually printed on the wrapper), particularly as regards to pressing.

- **Temporary fabric glue:** Look for a water-soluble product to secure your prepared fabric shapes to the background fabric until you're ready to appliqué them in place.

- **Spray starch and brush:** You'll need these items if you choose the spray-starch basting method (page 71) to prepare your fabric shapes for appliqué. You can use the generic spray starch found on the grocery store shelf in either regular or extra strength. Be sure you use starch; spray sizing doesn't seem to do the job as well. For the brush, you can use either a small paintbrush or small foam makeup brush.

- **Glue stick:** This is a must-have for the glue-stick basting method (page 73) of preparing your shapes for appliqué. The brand is unimportant so long as the glue is water soluble.

- **Pointed pressing tool:** If you are using the spray-starch basting method, in addition to a stiletto, you'll want a pointed tool that is a bit thicker and heavier for preparing any deep inside (V) angles. The 4-in-1 Essential Sewing Tool (see Stiletto and Seam Ripper, page 17) is a good choice for this task.

> **note**
>
> When referring to appliqué shapes, the terms *seam allowance* and *turn-under allowance* are used interchangeably.

- **Bias-tape maker:** When used with your iron, a bias-tape maker is a handy notion that enables you to make folded bias strips from any fabric you like. The tool comes in various sizes so you can make ready-to-stitch vines and stems in the width you need for your project.

- **Bias presser bars:** Bias presser bars are narrow bars, made from either metal or vinyl, that come in a variety of widths—typically, ⅛" to 1¾". Although the product name usually includes the word *bias*, you can use them for stems cut from the straight grain as well.

- **Fray Check:** Fray Check is a clear liquid that helps stop fraying on the raw edges of appliqué fabrics. It is especially helpful when you are appliquéing very sharp inner (V) curves, as for hearts and deep scallops, until you become confident with the security of your stitches. (Use a toothpick as an applicator; this helps you control the amount of the liquid.) Another option is June Tailor Fray Block (see Resources, page 174), which is available in a tube and dries somewhat softer than traditional Fray Check. As with marking tools, be sure to test any product first on the fabrics you intend to use.

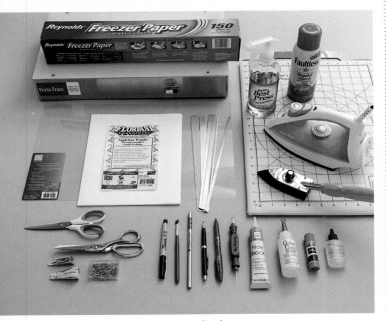

Tools needed for preparing appliqués

For Hand Appliqué

- **Thimble (if you normally use one for hand sewing)**

- **Thread:** In addition to the 50-weight, 100% cotton thread you use on your sewing machine, which comes in a variety of colors, you may want to try some of the *many* other threads available. The "Rolls Royce" choice is silk, which buries itself so well in the fabric you only need a couple of basic colors, such as light taupe, dark gray, and a few primary hues. However, silk thread can be expensive. A wonderful alternative is a high-end polyester such as Libby Lehman's The Bottom Line (see Resources, page 174). Embroidery floss and perle cotton are good choices for hand buttonhole appliqué.

- For most hand appliqué, your thread should match (or blend invisibly into) the color of your appliqué piece, not the background. Exceptions are noted when applicable.

- **Needles:** Various types of needles are available for hand appliqué, each with its own benefits. For the basic appliqué stitch (page 79), I recommend that you start with size 11 sharps; they're long, slender, easy to maneuver, and easy to find. Other options include straw or milliner's needles, which are slightly longer than sharps. On the other hand, if you're adept at hand quilting and are comfortable with a smaller needle, you might want to try a betweens quilting needle (see Needles, page 15) for your appliqué. For the hand buttonhole (or blanket) stitch, choose a needle with an eye large enough to accommodate one strand of perle cotton or two strands of embroidery floss and with a sharp point. Examples include a size 6–8 embroidery or sharps needle.

Needles and threads suitable for hand appliqué

For Machine Appliqué

- Sewing machine
- **Thread:** With machine appliqué, you have two thread choices to make: the thread that passes through the needle on top of the machine and the thread you wind on the bobbin. You'll also want to make the best possible choice for the technique you plan to use.

  Top thread: For invisible-stitch appliqué, use a quality invisible thread, such as MonoPoly, or a fine cotton, such as MasterPiece (see Resources, page 174), in a color to match the appliqué shape. Use jeans thread for the buttonhole (or blanket) stitch. Your choice of color for the buttonhole stitch will depend upon whether you want the stitches to be inconspicuous or you want them to contrast and act as a design element.

  Bobbin thread: My favorites for the blind hem-stitch (including free motion) are fine cotton, such as MasterPiece, or a high-end polyester, such as The Bottom Line (see Resources, page 174). For this technique, the bobbin thread should match the color of the background fabric. For the but-tonhole (or blanket) stitch, I prefer 50-weight cotton thread to match the top thread.

- **Needles:** The topstitch needle is my hands-down favorite for machine appliqué. It suits a variety of threads, and I don't need to think about what I have in my machine when I sit down to sew. It has a larger eye that is particularly kind to fragile (such as metallic) or other decorative threads. A jeans needle would be my go-to second choice.

- **Specialty feet:** You'll want to keep a few specialty feet close by. For invisible-stitch appliqué, use the open-toe embroidery foot (see Feet, page 11); it allows you to see ahead to where you are about to stitch and has a cut out V shape on the bottom that gives the stitch somewhere to go.

- **Stabilizer:** Stabilizer, which is similar to interfacing, helps keep your machine buttonhole (blanket) stitches from puckering. Choose a tear-away or wash-away version that you can remove easily after the appliqués are stitched or when the entire quilt is finished.

Needles, threads, and notions suitable for machine appliqué

PREPARING FOR APPLIQUÉ

Appliqué takes preparation, both for the individual appliqué shapes and for the appliqué background. This preparation isn't difficult; just read through the following pages to determine which methods work best for you and your particular project.

Detail of appliqué in *Flower Pops* (page 9)

> ### tip
>
> If you typically don't prewash your fabrics, you may want to reconsider it for both your hand- and machine-appliqué projects. In addition to removing any sizing, finishing chemicals, and excess dyes, prewashing makes the fabric more supple and the edges easier to turn. Also, some of the preparation methods involve spray starch or temporary fabric glues that you'll need to wash from the finished quilt.

Preparing Individual Appliqués (Hand or Machine)

There are a number of ways to prepare the individual fabric shapes. Some methods work for one specific appliqué technique; others work for multiple techniques. The following preparation methods are suitable for both hand and machine appliqué.

> ### tip
>
> When preparing finished-edge appliqué shapes for machine appliqué, a really firm ironing surface helps you achieve nice, crisp turned edges.

Preparing for Paper-Basted Appliqué

You'll need to *reverse the pattern* for any of the following paper-basted methods. When a shape will be overlapped with another shape, you do not need to prepare the raw edge that will be overlapped. These raw edges will typically be indicated on the pattern with dashed lines.

THREAD BASTING

For the thread-basting method, the freezer-paper template must remain in place while you stitch the appliqué shape to the background. Remove the template after the stitching is complete (see Cutting Away the Background, page 83).

1. Reverse the patterns given with the project and trace them onto the dull (paper) side of freezer paper. You'll need one freezer-paper template for each individual appliqué. Cut out the freezer-paper templates directly on the traced lines.

2. Place each freezer-paper template shiny side down on the wrong side of the appliqué fabric. Leave at least ½" between shapes to allow for the turn-under allowance. Press.

Place freezer paper onto the fabric and press.

3. Cut out the appliqué shapes, adding a scant ¼" (approximately ³⁄₁₆") for the turn-under allowance.

Cut out.

4. Roll the edge of the fabric over the paper template and baste with needle and thread.

Roll the edge of the fabric over freezer paper and baste.

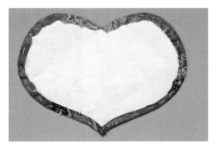

Wrong side

Right side

tip

For shapes with deep inside curves, use a very sharp scissors to clip just to the edge of the freezer paper. For added insurance, consider using a toothpick to apply a drop of Fray Check to the fabric.

Clip the inside curve.

SPRAY-STARCH BASTING METHOD

I *love* the spray-starch basting method; it's become my favorite way to prepare shapes for both hand and machine appliqué. Not only is it easy, but also the freezer paper is removed before the shape is stitched to the background, and you can reuse the paper templates many times. While you'll want to use one of the techniques described in Preparing Circles (page 73) to prepare your smallest round shapes, this spray-starch basting method works well for larger circles, too.

tip

You must be willing to immerse the finished project in water to remove the spray starch, as starch left in the fabric may attract silverfish.

1. Layer 2 pieces of freezer paper, shiny sides down, and press to adhere the layers. The double thickness gives more rigidity and makes it easier to turn over the edges. Reverse each pattern piece given with the project and trace it onto the dull (paper) side of the layered freezer paper. Cut out the freezer-paper templates on the traced lines.

2. Press the layered template shiny side down to the wrong side of the desired appliqué fabric. Cut out the fabric shape, adding a little less than ¼" (approximately ³⁄₁₆") turn-under allowance.

Press the template onto fabric and cut.

3. Spray a bit of spray starch into the cap from the starch. (Water down the starch a bit if you like.) Using a small paintbrush (or foam makeup brush) and working with the paper side up, apply the starch to the exposed turn-under allowance. Be sure to use enough starch to saturate the fabric.

4. Using a stiletto in one hand and a small wand iron in the other hand, coax the turn-under allowance over the edge of the freezer-paper template. When you are finished, turn over the prepared shape to check your results. Make any minor adjustments in the edges now; once the shape is thoroughly pressed (Step 6), it is difficult to make any adjustments.

Fold the turn-under allowance over the template.

5. When you've finished turning the edges, press the prepared appliqué thoroughly dry on both sides.

6. Lift a small edge of the turn-under allowance and remove the freezer paper. Re-press the shape to ensure that the starch is completely dry. Your shape is now ready to appliqué, and you can reuse the discarded template multiple times!

Remove the template.

tips

Here are some tips for coping with potentially tricky curves and angles when using the spray-starch technique.

For curves:

Don't try to press the entire curve in one motion. Instead, use the stiletto and the tip of the wand iron to create a ruffled edge around the curve. When you're satisfied that you've turned the curve cleanly, press the entire curve and continue.

Finesse fabric around the curve.

For deep inside (V) angles:

1. Use very sharp scissors to clip all the way to the edge of the paper template, directly toward the V.

2. Place a pointed tool, such as my 4-in-1 Essential Sewing Tool (see Stiletto and Seam Ripper, page 17), directly at the V. Keeping the point nestled tight against the V, pivot the tool's handle toward yourself.

3. Use the wand iron to carefully press the turn-under allowance in place on both sides of the V.

Clip the angle and press.

GLUE-STICK BASTING METHOD

Glue-stick basting is another simple method for paper basting shapes over freezer-paper templates. With this method, you'll need to make one template for each appliqué shape. The template remains in place while the shape is stitched to the background. The template is removed after the stitching is complete (see Cutting Away the Background, page 83).

1. Prepare the fabric shapes as described in Thread Basting, Steps 1–3 (page 70).

2. Using a water-soluble glue stick, apply glue to the turn-under allowance and roll the edge of the fabric over the paper template, using your fingers to maneuver the fabric smoothly over the template's edges.

Apply glue and roll the fabric over the template.

Smooth the fabric along the edges with your fingers.

3. After you've appliquéd the shapes using your preferred hand or machine method, cut away the backing fabric, leaving a ¼" seam allowance. Spritz with cool water to release the glue, and then remove the template (see Cutting Away the Background, page 83).

Preparing Circles

My favorite method for preparing circles for appliqué is the "shower cap" method.

1. Trace the circle pattern given with the project onto heat-resistant template material. Cut out the template on the traced lines. Go for perfection here; if the plastic circle is "wonky," your finished fabric circle will be, too.

> **tip**
>
> Precut circle templates come in a variety of sizes. You might want to check your local quilt shop or online source for the sizes you need. Another option: visit your local scrapbooking store and purchase a circle cutter—this tool makes quick work of cutting your own templates from heat-resistant plastic.

2. Place the circle template on the wrong side of the desired fabric. Use your preferred marker to trace around the template.

Trace the circle onto fabric.

3. Remove the template and cut out the fabric shape, adding a little less than ¼" (approximately ³⁄₁₆") turn-under allowance.

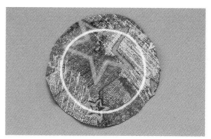

Cut out.

4. Knot one end of a single strand of sturdy thread. Beginning with a back-stitch, sew around the perimeter of the fabric circle with a running stitch, making sure to keep the stitching within the area between the traced line and the fabric circle's raw edge.

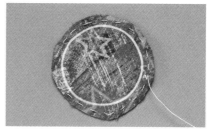

Sew.

5. Replace the template. Pull the thread to gather the fabric turn-under allowance around the template. Smooth out any folds, saturate the shape on both sides with spray starch, and use a *very hot steam* iron to press the fabric circle. Allow the starch to dry *completely*.

Pull the thread to gather.

6. Loosen the gathering thread and carefully remove the template. Once again, gently pull the gathering thread so the fabric forms a perfect circle.

Loosen the thread and remove the template.

Preparing for Raw-Edge Appliqué

The raw-edge appliqué method is used to prepare appliqué shapes for hand or machine buttonhole (blanket) stitch. With this method, you do not add a seam allowance to the appliqué shapes. The shapes are prepared using a lightweight fusible web and are bonded to the background with an iron. As you did for the paper-basting preparation method, you will need to *reverse the pattern* for the raw-edge appliqué method.

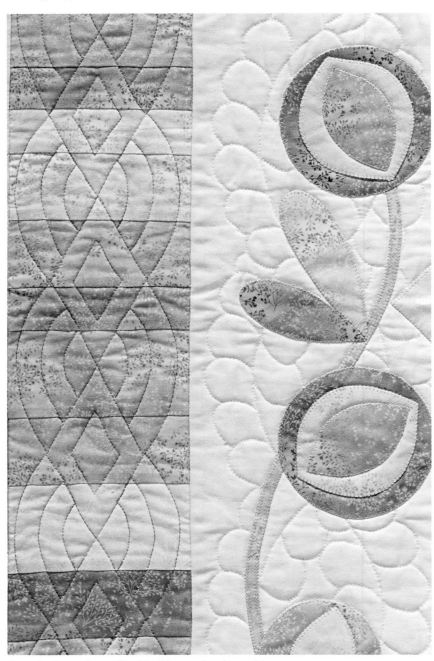

Example of raw-edge appliqué, in this case, done by machine

OPTION 1: USING A TEMPLATE

1. To make a set of templates, reverse each pattern given with the project and trace it onto sturdy template material. Cut out the templates on the traced lines.

2. Follow the manufacturer's directions to bond the fusible web to the wrong side of the desired appliqué fabric.

3. Place the template on the paper side of the fusible web that you fused to the fabric in Step 2. Trace around the template with a sharp pencil.

Trace the shape.

4. Cut out the appliqué shape on the traced line.

Cut out.

OPTION 2: TRACING THE SHAPE

1. Reverse each pattern given with the project and trace it onto the paper side of fusible web.

2. Cut out each shape approximately ¼" from the drawn line.

Trace the shape onto fusible web and cut out.

3. Follow the manufacturer's directions to bond the fusible web to the wrong side of the desired appliqué fabric.

Fuse to the fabric.

4. Cut out the appliqué shape on the traced line.

Cut out.

---

tip

If you're bothered or concerned by the stiffness of fused appliqués, try this: *Before* pressing the fusible to the appliqué fabric, trim away the center of the fusible shape, leaving a ¼" seam allowance. This is especially helpful for large appliqué pieces.

Preparing Vines and Stems

For curving stems and vines, cut strips on the bias, or the diagonal grain of the fabric (see Fabric Grain, page 18). Bias strips stretch nicely to create curves. For straight stems, which don't need to bend, you can cut the necessary strips from the straight (lengthwise or crosswise) grain of the fabric.

> **tip**
>
> When piecing multiple strips for vines, join the strips with diagonal seams (see Cutting and Grainline, page 104). Press the joining seams in one direction so that the bar doesn't get hung up in the seam allowances.

USING THE SEW-AND-FLIP METHOD

Formula: Cut a bias strip twice the desired width of the finished strip plus ½".

1. Cut bias strips to the width and length listed in the project cutting instructions. With wrong sides together, fold the strip in half lengthwise and press.

2. Hand or machine stitch the strip ¼" from the raw edges directly onto the background fabric.

Fold the strip in half, press, and stitch.

3. Carefully press the folded edge of the strip over the seam, so the strip covers the raw edges. If the strip is not wide enough to cover the raw edge, trim the seam allowance if necessary.

Press and trim if necessary.

4. Use your preferred appliqué stitch to stitch the folded edge in place.

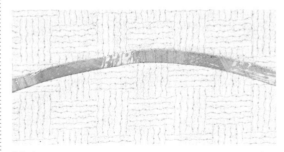

Stitch.

USING A BIAS-TAPE MAKER

Formula: Cut a bias strip twice the desired width of the finished strip.

Bias-tape makers come in a variety of sizes. Choose one that will give you the finished size you desire. My advice is to follow the instructions on the packaging of the bias-tape maker; however, here are a few tips to help you along.

■ Cut the leading end of the strip at an angle so it is easier to feed into the tool.

■ Spray the strip *lightly* with spray starch and crumble the strip gently in your hands to distribute the starch evenly.

■ Use a stiletto to maneuver the strip.

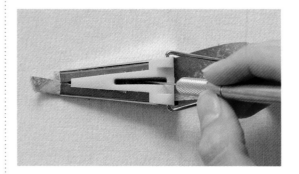

Secure the angled end of the strip to your ironing board with a straight pin. With one hand holding the iron over the folded end, gently pull the tool across the fabric strip with your other hand, pressing the strip into shape.

After you've used the tool, use straight pins to coax the prepared strips into gentle curves on your ironing surface.

USING BIAS PRESSER BARS

Formula: Cut a bias strip at least twice the width of the bias presser bar plus a scant ⅝″ for metal bars or a generous ⅝″ for vinyl bars.

1. Cut bias strips to the width and length listed in the project cutting instructions. If necessary, piece the strips with diagonal seams to achieve the required length (page 105).

2. With wrong sides together, fold the strip in half lengthwise and press. Carefully sew a seam ¼″ from the long raw edge.

3. Insert the desired bias presser bar into the fabric tube and roll the seam to the underside of the bar, trimming the seam if necessary. Press the strip (I like to use steam). After each section is pressed, move the bar down the fabric tube and press again. Take care if you are using a metal bias presser bar because it will get very hot.

Roll the seam to the underside and press.

Preparing Individual Appliqués (Hand Only)

The techniques in this section are suitable for hand appliqué.

Preparing for Needle-Turn Appliqué

1. To make a set of templates, trace each pattern given with the project onto sturdy template material. Cut out the templates directly on the traced lines.

2. Place each template on the right side of the appropriate appliqué fabric. Trace around the template with your preferred removable marking tool.

Trace around the template.

3. Cut out the appliqué shape, adding a little less than ¼″ (approximately ³⁄₁₆″) turn-under allowance.

Cut out the shape.

Preparing the Background for Appliqué (Hand or Machine)

I recommend that you cut your background blocks slightly oversized (1″–2″ larger) to accommodate the slight shrinkage, or drawing up, that can occur as you appliqué the shapes.

1. Mark the center point of the background block and the vertical and horizontal (and sometimes the diagonal) axis points. These guidelines are extremely helpful in positioning the appliqués on the background area. You can mark the background block by folding it in half vertically and then creasing it with your fingers or by using a pressing tool, such as my 4-in-1 Essential Sewing Tool (see Resources, page 174) or an iron (lightly). Unfold the block. Repeat this step to fold and crease the block horizontally and, if desired, along both diagonals. You can also use this same vertical/horizontal folding method to "mark" border strips for appliqué.

> I don't mark the design on the background. Instead, I either eyeball the placement of the appliqués or use a lightbox to position and glue the appliqué shapes in place using water-soluble fabric glue.

2. Layer the appliqué pieces from the bottom up; that is, in the order you'll be stitching them. Place a few dots of the temporary fabric glue around the edges on the wrong side of each shape (and a few in the center, if you like) and gently finger-press the shape to the background.

Place temporary fabric glue.

3. Layer the shapes as appropriate.

Layer the shapes.

4. Once you've finished with the appliqué, trim the block to the finished size *plus ¼″ seam allowance* all around, making sure to keep the appliqué design centered in the block.

> When preparing a motif with many layers, stitch the layers together before you appliqué the shape to the quilt top. Handling the small pieces in this way is easier than trying to stitch them to the larger quilt background.

HAND-APPLIQUÉ TECHNIQUES

If you love the meditative quality of handwork, this is for you! Read through the options, choose an appropriate preparation method from the previous section, and enjoy the process. A small lap desk, like the type you might find in a book or stationery store, makes a great surface for hand appliqué. Make sure you have ample light, and stop occasionally to rest your eyes and to stretch and flex your fingers.

Basic Appliqué Stitch

Note: Typically, if you're right-handed, you'll stitch right to left, or counterclockwise. Lefties usually stitch in the reverse direction: left to right, or clockwise. The photos show you both ways.

The following instructions for the basic appliqué stitch are the same for needle-turn or paper-basted appliqué. The difference is that with needle-turn appliqué, you turn under the seam allowances as you stitch the shapes to the background, whereas with paper-basted appliqué, the raw edges are turned under before you stitch the shape to the background. The instructional photos show the needle-turn method.

> **tip**
>
> If you've used the thread-basted (page 70) or glue-stick (page 73) preparation techniques, you'll need to remove the freezer-paper templates after the shapes have been stitched to the background. Remove the basting threads or moisten the shape to loosen the glue. Use a small sharp-pointed scissors to make a slit in the background fabric behind the appliqué shape, as described in Cutting Away the Background (page 83). Remove the freezer-paper template. If you wish, cut away the background fabric inside the shape, leaving a little less than ¼˝ (approximately ³⁄₁₆˝) seam allowance.

Needle-Turn Appliqué

1. Thread your needle with a single strand, knotting the end. The best place to start stitching is on a straight or slightly curved edge. Fold under the edge of the shape on the marked line at the point where you will begin stitching. Turn under only the amount of fabric you can control and stitch at one time (about ½˝). From the back of the shape, come through the fabric exactly at the folded edge you want to stitch. The knot will be hidden behind the fabric.

For lefties

For righties

2. Reinsert the needle straight down into the background fabric, right beside the point at which the needle emerged. Travel approximately ⅛˝ under the background fabric, and then come back up again through the background fabric and the folded edge. Ideally, you want to catch the underside of the fold so the stitch is hidden under the fold. To complete the stitch, pull the thread just taut—not too tight, not too loose.

3. Continue using the tip of the needle to turn the edge of the fabric under as you go.

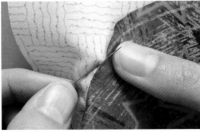

For lefties

For righties

4. When you're finished stitching the appliqué shape, insert the needle straight down into the background fabric and pull the needle so the thread is taut. Take a tiny stitch in the background fabric behind the appliqué shape, as close as possible to the last appliqué stitch.

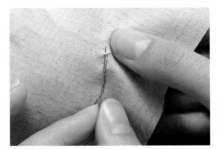

For lefties

For righties

5. Wrap the thread around the needle twice, and then pull the thread through the wraps.

6. Insert the needle through the background fabric between the appliqué and the background layers. Come up about ½" from the insertion point. Carefully trim off the thread. The tail will be hidden between the layers.

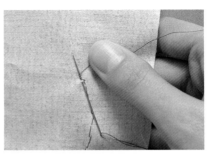

For lefties

For righties

For pressing the finished appliqué block, use a soft, giving surface, such as a fluffy towel folded double. Press from the reverse side of the block so you don't smoosh the appliqués flat. This is true for pressing finished machine appliqué blocks as well.

Curves

Use small sharp-pointed scissors to clip the inside curved edge of the turn-under allowance just to the marked line. The tighter the curve, the more clips you will need to make. As you appliqué the curve, make the stitches even closer together than usual.

For lefties

For righties

Points

1. Stitch up to the marked point using the basic appliqué stitch (page 79). When you reach the point, bring the needle up through the background and the appliqué shape, right at the tip of the marked point.

For lefties

For righties

2. Take a stitch exactly at the point.

For lefties

For righties

3. If necessary, carefully trim away a bit of the excess seam allowance underneath the area of the appliqué shape that you just stitched. The sharper the point, the smaller you will want the seam allowance to be.

For lefties

For righties

4. Use the tip of your needle to gently turn under the seam allowance on the other side of the point. (Turning the seam allowance under at the point should require 2 or more stitches.) Take an extra stitch to anchor the point, pulling the thread taut (not tight) to help define the point. Continue stitching away from the point with the basic appliqué stitch.

For lefties

For righties

Inside (V) Angles

1. Starting on a straight or slightly curved edge, use the basic appliqué stitch (page 79) to begin sewing the appliqué shape to the background. Stop stitching just before you reach the V. Use a very sharp scissors to clip all the way to the marked turn-under line, directly toward the V.

2. Take 1 or 2 tiny anchoring stitches right at the V to keep the clipped turn-under allowance from fraying. (Fray Check can help here.)

For lefties

For righties

3. Resume stitching on the other side of the V with the basic appliqué stitch.

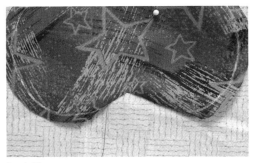

For lefties

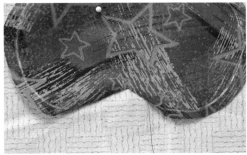

For righties

Buttonhole-Stitch (Blanket-Stitch) Appliqué

With buttonhole-stitch appliqué, there are no seam allowances to turn under, and the result is less formal looking than that achieved with the needle-turn and paper-basted methods. You can choose threads to match the appliqués for a subtle effect or have fun introducing threads in contrasting colors to add an extra layer of design.

1. Thread your needle with 1 strand of perle cotton or 2 strands of embroidery floss. Knot the thread.

2. Bring the threaded needle up through the raw edge of the appliqué fabric. Hold the thread down and out of the way with your thumb and reinsert the needle into the appliqué shape approximately ⅛″ from the previous stitch. Reemerge at the raw edge of the appliqué, bringing the tip of the needle over the working thread. Pull the thread taut (not tight) to bring the stitch into place. Continue stitching in this manner all the way around the shape.

For lefties

For righties

3. Knot off.

Points and Inside V Angles

When you reach a point or corner, make a small anchor stitch before proceeding to the adjacent side.

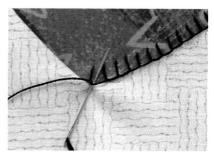
For lefties

For righties

Cutting Away the Background

Once the appliqué piece is finished, you'll need to decide whether to cut away the background fabric behind the sewn shapes. If the piece is small, dark, and only one layer deep, such as a small leaf, I tend not to bother. However, if the shape is multilayered or if an underlying layer has the possibility of shadowing through, cutting away the background is a sensible step. Use a small sharp-pointed scissors to make a slit in the background fabric behind the appliqué shape. Cut away the background fabric inside the shape, leaving a little less than ¼″ (approximately ³⁄₁₆″) seam allowance.

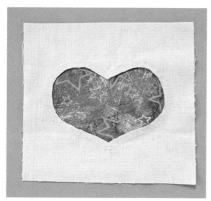
Cut away the background.

Reverse Appliqué

As its name implies, this technique is the reverse of traditional appliqué. Rather than stitching the appliqué piece on top of another fabric, with reverse appliqué, you layer the fabrics in such a way that when you cut away the top fabric in the desired shape, you reveal the appliqué fabric underneath. When your appliqué includes rounded shapes or shapes that you simply want to recede, reverse appliqué may be the answer.

Examples of reverse appliqué can be seen in the eye and in some of the feather detailing.

1. Trace the pattern for the piece that you plan to reverse appliqué onto sturdy template material. Cut out the template directly on the traced lines.

2. Place the template on the right side of the *top* fabric and trace around the shape with your preferred (non-permanent) marking tool.

3. Cut out the shape *inside* the traced line, leaving a little less than ¼″ (approximately ³⁄₁₆″) turn-under allowance. Layer the top fabric over the fabric you want to reveal and pin or baste.

Cut out.

4. Use thread to match the *top* fabric and the needle-turn method (see Basic Appliqué Stitch, page 79) to turn under and stitch the top fabric to the underlying layer.

Stitch.

MACHINE-APPLIQUÉ TECHNIQUES

With the innovations in sewing machine technology and with the wide variety of threads and notions available, machine appliqué is easier and more rewarding than ever. Refer to Preparing the Background for Appliqué (page 78) as needed.

Invisible-Stitch Appliqué

With this technique, the edges of the appliqués are turned before they are stitched. With a just a little practice, you can give your machine work the look of beautiful hand-stitched appliqué.

An example of invisible machine appliqué; the complete quilt appears on the cover of my book, *Hand and Machine Appliqué with Alex Anderson.*

Machines made by different manufacturers have different stitches to accomplish the invisible-stitch appliqué. For example, on your machine, the stitch might be called the blind hemstitch, the overlock stitch, the hand-look appliqué stitch, or something similar.

Refer to your machine's manual and become familiar with what your machine can do. The key is to find a stitch that will take a few (two to three) small straight stitches along the outer edge of the appliqué shape and then take a bite into and out of the shape before continuing. You may want to shorten the stitch length and narrow the stitch a bit; you want the bite to be as small as possible but still secure the appliqué shape.

I like to set my needle to the far-right position and use the inside edge of the presser foot as a guide. Depending upon your machine, doing so may require that you mirror-image the stitch.

1. Attach the open-toe foot to your machine. Choose the appropriate stitch on your machine and make any necessary adjustments.

2. Starting on a straight or slightly curved edge, position the needle right over the spot where you plan to start stitching. Lower the presser foot. Holding onto the top thread, take a complete stitch, so that the needle returns to its highest position. In the following photographs, contrasting thread was used so that the stitches would be visible. Your thread should match your appliqué shape.

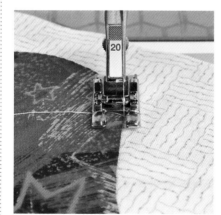

Take a complete stitch.

3. Without raising the presser foot, gently tug the top thread to pull a loop of bobbin thread to the fabric surface. Pull the tail of the bobbin thread through to the surface.

Pull the top thread to bring the bobbin thread to the surface.

tip

If your bobbin hook has an eye, thread the bobbin thread through it. This helps pull down the top thread, enhancing the look of the finished stitch.

4. Engage the needle-down feature, if your machine has one. Insert the needle into the background, fabric right beside the shape, and begin stitching. The machine will take a few small straight stitches and will then take a V-shaped bite into the appliqué shape.

Stitch.

5. To end, pull the thread tails through to the back and tie them off. Or you can reduce the stitch length to 0, take a few stitches in place, and carefully trim the thread tails. While your stitches may be visible at this stage, they will become virtually invisible once the quilt is machine quilted.

Points

For a point (or on an outside corner), stitch right to the tip of the point, making sure to stop with the needle down on the *inside* edge of the appliqué, having taken the first half of the V-shaped bite. Lift the presser foot, pivot, lower the foot, and resume stitching on the other side of the point.

Points

Inside V Angles

For an inside V angle, stitch right to the angle, this time making sure to stop with the needle down on the *outside* edge of the appliqué shape, immediately after taking the second half of the V-shaped bite. Lift the presser foot, pivot, lower the foot, and resume stitching on the other side of the angle.

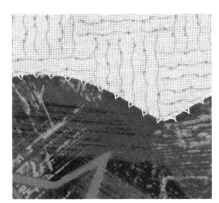

Inside V angles

Customizing Stitches

Another option for machine, *finished-edge* appliqué is to use the blanket stitch with the bite shortened to 1.0 and the length at 4.0. This results in a very tiny bite, which virtually disappears.

note

The stitch settings given above are based on my BERNINA; you may need to play around a bit to achieve similar results on your machine.

tip

If your machine has two spool pins and the top thread is stacked on the spool, use the vertical spool pin. If the thread is cross-wound (crisscrossed), use the horizontal spool pin.

Cross-wound spool (left), stacked spool (right)

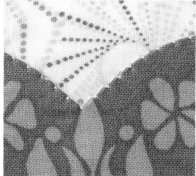

An example of customized stitching— I used white thread so the stitching would be more visible.

Raw-Edge Appliqué with Buttonhole (or Blanket) Stitch

This technique has all the benefits of its hand counterpart, but you do the stitch by machine instead. Experiment to find the stitch width and length that gives you the desired result, keeping in mind the size of the appliqué shapes. If you prefer, substitute a satin stitch or one of the other decorative stitches on your machine for the buttonhole (blanket) stitch. Just make sure you choose a foot suited for the stitch.

Example of raw-edge appliqué with a machine buttonhole stitch

1. Back the area behind the appliqué with a tear-away or wash-away stabilizer (page 69) to keep the stitches from puckering.

2. Attach the open-toe foot to your machine. Move the machine needle to the far-right position and select the buttonhole stitch on your machine. Set the stitch length and width as desired. If necessary, reverse the direction of the stitch. Pull up the bobbin thread and engage the needle-down feature.

3. Starting on a straight or slightly curved edge, insert the needle into the background fabric. Reduce the stitch length to 0 and take a few stitches.

Stitch.

4. Return to the desired stitch length and continue stitching.

5. Finish off as described in Invisible-Stitch Appliqué, Step 5 (page 86).

Points

1. For a point (or an outside corner), stop stitching as you approach the point and use the hand wheel for control as you make the next few stitches, finishing on the shape's *outside* edge. You may need to manipulate both the stitch and the background fabric a bit so the needle enters the fabric exactly at the point.

Stop stitching at the point.

2. Leaving the needle in the down position, pivot the fabric and take the bite stitch so that it divides the angle in half.

Pivot and make a stitch at the point.

3. Return the needle to the background fabric, pivot, and continue stitching.

Inside V Angles

1. For an inside V angle, stop stitching when your needle enters the background fabric at the inside angle. Once again, you may need to manipulate both the stitch *and* the background fabric so that the needle enters at the correct place.

Stop stitching at the inside angle.

2. Leaving the needle in the down position, pivot the fabric and take the bite stitch so that it divides the inside V angle in half.

Pivot and make a stitch at the inside angle.

3. Return the needle to the background fabric, pivot, and continue stitching.

PUTTING IT TOGETHER:
SETTINGS
AND BORDERS

Once you've made a bunch of blocks, it's time to put them on your design wall and assess what you've got. This is when your quilt will really begin to "speak" to you, to make its needs and preferences known—and it's always a good idea to listen.

WHAT YOU'LL NEED

- Rotary cutter
- Rotary mat
- Rotary rulers
- Sewing machine
- Thread
- Pins
- Marking tools
- Iron and pressing station
- Design wall
- Freezer paper (optional)

SETTINGS

There are loads of options for setting your quilt, and I encourage you—even if you've had a plan in mind from the very beginning—to experiment before making the final commitment to sew the blocks together. Use your design wall (see Design Wall, page 13) to play with shifting, staggering, and rotating the blocks. In some cases, you'll discover wonderful surprises.

> **tip**
>
> Sometimes unexpected secondary designs appear when blocks go up on the design wall.

Photo by Ken Wagner

Memories of Monet (70½″ × 70½″) designed and made by Joen Wolfrom, machine quilted by Veronica Nurmi

Gallery of Settings

Here are just a few of the possibilities you can try.

Straight (or block-to-block) set: For this simple set, blocks are set side by side, edges touching, in vertical and horizontal rows.

Star Party (72″ × 80″) designed and made by Alex Anderson, machine quilted by Paula Reid

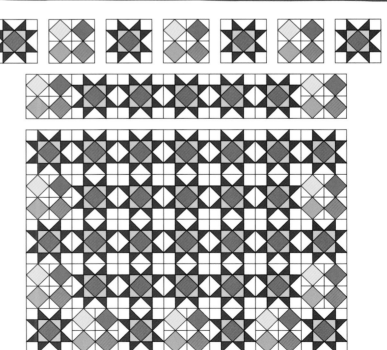

Diagonal set: In this set, blocks are turned "on point" or "on their ears." This set can breathe new life into old favorite blocks, particularly those made completely from squares, such as the Four-Patch and Nine-Patch. Others, such as Basket and Tree blocks, seem naturally designed to be set this way.

Blocks are sewn together in diagonal rows that are finished with side and corner setting triangles to square up the quilt center—another opportunity to add fun fabrics to the mix.

Hot Flash
(58½″ × 61″)
designed and made
by Alex Anderson,
machine quilted
by Paula Reid

Photo by Gregory Case

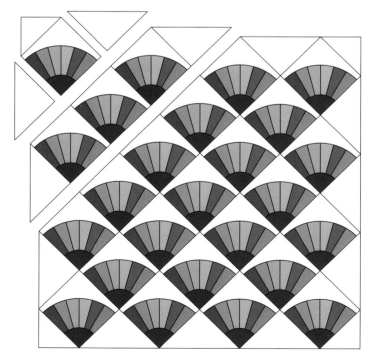

■ THE MAGIC NUMBER FOR DIAGONAL SETS

When working with on-point blocks and sets, you'll need to know the measurement across the block, from point to point, as well as the usual side measurement. This point-to-point measurement helps you determine the size of the quilt center when the blocks are sewn into diagonal rows, as well as how to size the required setting triangles. This info will also help you size setting triangles for the Zigzag or Streak of Lightning set (page 96).

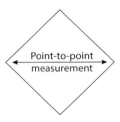

Happily, there is another Magic Number to help with these calculations. That number is 1.414.

To determine the block's point-to-point measurement, multiply the finished side of the block by 1.414. For a 12" finished block, the point-to-point measurement would be 12" × 1.414 = 16.968", which rounds up nicely to 17".

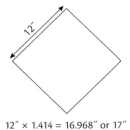

12" × 1.414 = 16.968" or 17"

Sizing the Setting Triangles

The size of the setting triangles you'll need for your diagonally set quilt is based on the finished size of the diagonally set blocks. Let's use our 12" finished block as an example.

Side setting triangles:

Since it's always a good idea to place the straight of grain (rather than the stretchy bias) along the outside edge of your quilt center, you'll cut the side setting triangles from squares divided into quarter-square triangles. This places the long diagonal edge of the triangle on the straight of grain (see Fabric Grain, page 18), exactly where you want it to be.

We've already used our 1.414 Magic Number to determine that the diagonal measurement of a 12" block is 17".

We also know that 1¼" is the Magic Number we must add to the square to yield four properly sized quarter-square triangles (see Quarter-Square Triangles, page 41). In this case, the square must measure 18¼" (17" + 1¼" = 18¼").

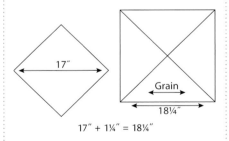

17" + 1¼" = 18¼"

Corner setting triangles:

In a diagonally set quilt, these four triangles are placed with their short, right-angle sides along the outside edges, so it is on these sides that we want the straight of grain to fall. This means you'll cut the corner setting triangles from squares divided into half-square triangles.

We know the finished size of the block is 12". The same Magic Number— 1.414—applies, but this time we'll divide, rather than multiply, to find the size square we need to cut.

Here's the simple math: 12" ÷ 1.414 = 8.487", which rounds nicely to 8½".

We also know that ⅞" is the Magic Number we must add to the square to yield the two properly sized half-square triangles (see Half-Square Triangles, page 41). In this case, the square must measure 9⅜" (8½" + ⅞" = 9⅜").

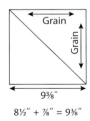

8½" + ⅞" = 9⅜"

To help you get started, the chart shows the diagonal (point-to-point) measurements for the most commonly sized blocks, rounded to the nearest ¹⁄₁₆".

Finished block size	Diagonal measurement
3"	4¼"
3½"	5"
4"	5⅝"
4½"	6⅜"
5"	7¹⁄₁₆"
5½"	7¾"
6	8½"
6½"	9³⁄₁₆"
7"	9⅞"
7½"	10⅝"
8"	11⁵⁄₁₆"
8½"	12"
9"	12¾"
9½"	13⁷⁄₁₆"
10"	14⅛"
10½"	14⅞"
11"	15⁹⁄₁₆"
11½"	16¼"
12"	17"
12½"	17¹¹⁄₁₆"
13"	18⅜"
14"	19³⁄₁₆"
15"	21¼"
16"	22⅝"
18"	25⅞"

Alternate-block or sashed set: Inserting plain blocks or sashing strips between the blocks is a good option if you feel your quilt needs some breathing space. The addition of cornerstones introduces another possibility for a secondary design (see *Popsicle Treat*, page 94). You can use these options for both straight-set and diagonally set quilts.

Charming Checks (39" × 53") designed and made by Sandy Klop at American Jane

Photo by Ken Wagner

Popsicle Treat
(46" × 46")
designed and made
by Alex Anderson,
machine quilted
by Pam Vieira-McGinnis

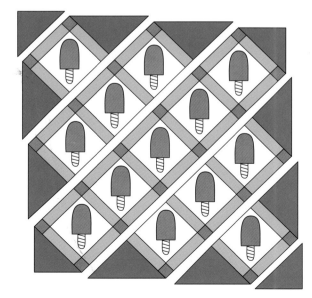

Strippie set: In this set, blocks are arranged in vertical (or horizontal) rows with strips of fabric in between. Blocks can be straight set or on point. You might even piece those setting strips (Flying Geese are fun) or add appliquéd vines or other simple motifs.

All a Flutter
(61″ × 51″)
designed and made
by Alex Anderson,
machine quilted
by Dianne Schweickert

Zigzag or Streak of Lightning set: In this set, blocks are turned on point and joined in vertical (or horizontal) rows that are finished with quarter- and half-square setting triangles. The stair-step effect is created by starting odd-numbered rows with quarter-square triangles and even-numbered rows with half-square triangles (see The Magic Number for Diagonal Sets, page 92).

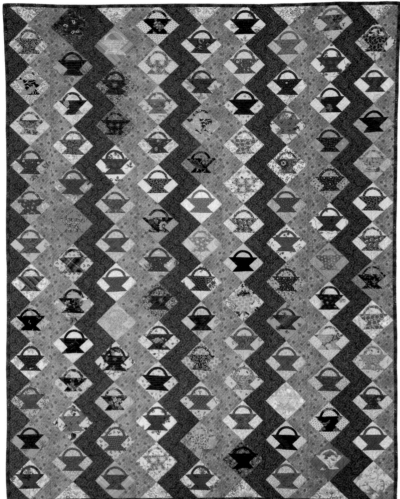

Little Basket (45½" × 62") by Edyta Sitar, quilted by Pat Loux

Photo by Edyta Sitar

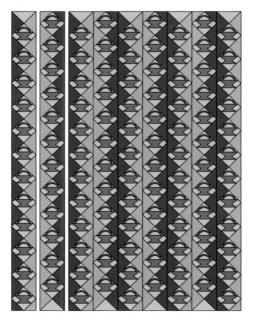

Staggered set: You can create a wonderful sense of movement in your quilt by staggering the blocks from row to row. You can accomplish this by starting and ending alternate rows with half of a pieced block (half the finished length of the block, plus ½" seam allowance), as shown in my quilt *Holiday Lights*. For an even easier option, start and end alternate rows with a plain (that is, unpieced) block that is half the length of the finished pieced block, plus ½" seam allowance.

Holiday Lights
(48" × 52")
designed by
Alex Anderson,
made and machine
quilted by
Elizabeth Schlarb

Randomly staggered set: Blocks don't need to line up in perfect rows, nor do they need to be the same size, though it does help to choose blocks that are mathematically compatible—for example, blocks that can be divided into units or increments of 2". If necessary, you can use filler strips or squares to fill the gaps. Just be sure to divide things so that you can sew larger sections—or neighborhoods— together with straight-line seams.

Welcome Home (63" × 63") designed and made by Alex Anderson, machine quilted by Paula Reid

Photo by Ken Wagner

Medallion set: In this set, a strong central motif (pieced, appliquéd, or a combination of both) is surrounded by a series of complementary borders. The borders can be a mix of pieced, plain (unpieced), or appliqué … whatever best suits the overall design.

Stars for Sue
(78″ × 78″)
designed and made
by Sue Garman

■ TROUBLESHOOTING: SOLVING SETTING SNAFUS

- If you have a block with a "what was I thinking" fabric or color, offset it—in the lower right quarter of the setting, for example—and then repeat that fabric or color in two other blocks, scattering them elsewhere around the quilt.

- Grouping the darker blocks in the bottom half of the setting grounds a quilt and gives it weight, as the lighter blocks above appear free to float away. Reverse this arrangement—darker blocks on top, lighter on the bottom, and the quilt may seem top heavy, trapping those lighter blocks below.

- Are your blocks looking too "samey"? Try mixing in a few more boisterous blocks. Blocks running wild? Maybe a few predictable, easy-to-read, high-contrast blocks are what you need. A single oddball block or color jumping out at you? Make a few more blocks, repeating that standout element, and spread them out so they flow seamlessly into the mix. The eye will absorb these mavericks along with the rest of the blocks as it skims the quilt surface, reading the design from the majority of the blocks or the ones that follow the rules.

- Here's a little tip I learned from friend and quilter Diana McClun: Place high-contrast blocks in the four corners of a scrap-quilt top to reinforce the design.

- There may be times when a block or two just won't fit, no matter how hard you try. Don't be afraid to remove the block from the design. You can always set it aside for a future project or—better still—incorporate it into the backing of the quilt you're making.

BORDERS

A quilt's border acts as a frame, and you'll want to choose an option (or options) that shows your quilt to its best advantage.

To be successful, the border treatment should make sense visually; that is, it should relate to or add something to the quilt's overall design. Use it to repeat or emphasize a key color, fabric, block, or other element in the body (center) of the quilt.

*Wagon Wheels
(75" × 75")
designed and made
by Sandy Klop
at American Jane*

Once again, your design wall (see Design Wall, page 13) is invaluable in deciding how to border your quilt. Use it to audition border ideas, including how wide to make the borders, and to make appropriate and effective fabric choices.

There's no rule that says quilts must have four identical borders. Quilts sometimes have borders on just two or three sides, or borders cut from different fabrics, or top and bottom borders that are wider (or narrower) than the side borders. Sometimes you'll even discover that your quilt doesn't need any borders at all.

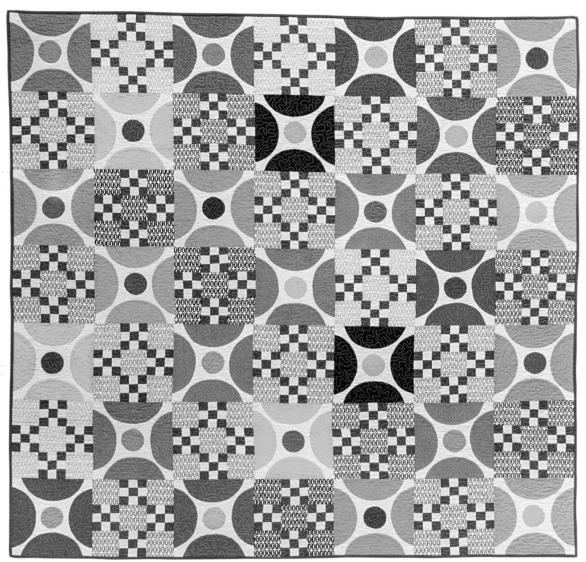

Pezzy Pizzaz
(63" × 63")
designed and made
by Sandy Klop
at American Jane

Design Considerations and Proportions

While there is no set rule for sizing borders, consider the size of the blocks, as well as the overall body of the quilt, and keep the borders in reasonable proportion.

Never use a border just to enlarge your quilt! It may seem like an easy way to stretch a minimum number of blocks, but the borders will overpower your quilt, and your strategy will be obvious. Instead, make those few extra blocks or try an alternative setting to maximize the blocks at hand. Your quilt is worth the effort.

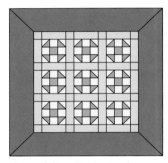
This quilt has pleasing borders.

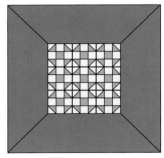
The border here is too large for the size and number of blocks.

Many quilts benefit from more than one border. The inner border is usually narrow in relation to the outer border(s), much like an inner mat on a framed picture. This look can give the eye a great resting place in the quilt's design and, on occasion, come in handy for making minor math adjustments between the body of the quilt and its outer borders. In addition, a pieced inner border can add visual interest to a "quiet" quilt.

If you decide to use multiple borders, vary their widths. Go from narrow to wider to wider still to narrow again. Once again, proportion is the key.

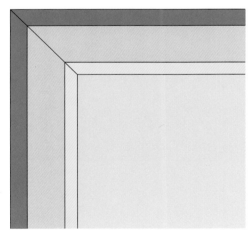
Vary the border widths.

tip

Some of my favorite inner borders are made from lively striped fabrics.

Pineapples (42″ × 50½″)
designed and made by Alex Anderson,
machine quilted by Paula Reid

Intended Use

When making a quilt for a bed, it's common to design the body of the quilt to cover the mattress top (see Standard Mattress Sizes, page 9) and the border(s) to form the overhang.

The typical drop for a bed-sized quilt is 10" on three sides: left, right, and bottom. If you have an extradeep mattress, measure to make sure that 10" will cover it. Some quilters also add 10" to account for the pillow, either by extending the design of the body of the quilt, by adding an extrawide sashing for a pillow tuck, or by adding a border to the top edge of the quilt as well.

Squaring Up the Quilt

If the corners of your quilt are not perfectly square, fix that before adding any borders. Use a large ruler to make sure the sides of your quilt top are straight and each corner forms a perfect 90° angle. Use your rotary cutter to make any adjustments. Be careful not to trim off important design elements, such as points, in the process.

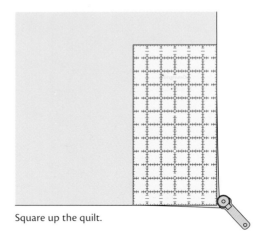

Square up the quilt.

Measuring for Borders

The edges of your quilt top may stretch a bit during the construction process. If you cut borders to match these slightly skewed outer-edge measurements, you'll end up with a bad case of wavy borders.

To avoid this problem, measure your quilt top *through its center*, both horizontally and vertically, rather than along its outside edges. Then use these "true" measurements to cut the borders.

> **tip**
>
> If my quilt is large, I measure two or three places on each side of the center and average these measurements to determine the border length.

Cutting and Grainline

It's a good idea to cut border strips before cutting any of the other pieces for your quilt. That way, you're sure to have enough fabric and won't need to piece odd leftovers to make the borders or—worse yet—discover there aren't enough leftovers to piece.

I allow a little extra length when cutting border strips for my quilts. Then I can measure the completed quilt top and trim the strips to size when I'm ready to stitch them.

You can cut border strips from either the lengthwise or crosswise grain of the fabric (see Fabric Grain, page 18). To cut borders from the crosswise grain, you'll generally need to purchase less yardage. Also, the slight give in the grain makes these borders easier to ease, or gently stretch to fit, than lengthwise-cut borders. You may need to piece strips to get the necessary length. Nondescript, subtle, tone-on-tone, or random prints work best for seamed borders. If your border fabric has a very distinctive print that will make seams obvious or if you just prefer borders without seams, purchase extra fabric and cut the borders from the lengthwise grain.

Certain fabrics are so obviously directional (for example, some pictorial prints) that you may wish to cut two borders on the crosswise grain and two on the lengthwise grain so that everything points "right side up." This may take additional yardage, which you'll want to know in advance ... it's also another good reason to audition fabrics on your design wall.

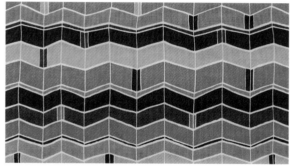

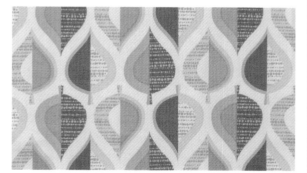

Examples of directional fabric

Whenever possible, I piece border strips with a diagonal seam. This distributes the visual weight of the seam so it tends to be less obvious. I make an exception for borders cut from striped fabrics, where a straight seam may be less noticeable.

To piece a diagonal seam:

1. Place 2 border strips right sides together, overlapping the ends at a 90° angle and allowing a ¼" overhang at the end of each strip.

2. Use a ruler to make a 45° angle on the top strip.

3. Sew on the marked line to join the strips.

4. Trim the excess fabric to a ¼" seam allowance and press the seam open.

5. Trim the "bunny ears" even with the strip edges.

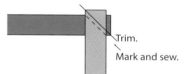

Piece the border strips.

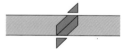

Trim the "bunny ears."

Each border treatment has its own requirements for figuring border lengths. You'll find this information in the section describing each specific technique.

Stitching Borders

1. Find and mark the midpoint on each side edge of the squared quilt top and the midpoint of each border strip by folding each in half and creasing lightly. For large quilts, mark additional points between the midpoints.

note

For some border options—such as mitered borders (page 107)—you'll also need to identify and mark the place where the border must match up with the corner of the quilt top. This is noted in the section describing that option.

2. Place the border and the quilt top right sides together. Match and pin the midpoints, corners, and any other marked key points. Fill in the "gaps" with as many pins as you need to distribute the fabric evenly, easing the quilt top to fit the border.

3. Stitch the border to the quilt top with a ¼" seam, checking periodically to be sure that you aren't stitching pleats into either the quilt top or the border.

4. Press the border seam. These seams are usually pressed away from the center of the quilt. Sometimes, however, they just want to go the other way, and I normally let the quilt take the lead.

tip

If your border requires a fair amount of easing, machine baste it to the quilt top first. Once you're sure that you haven't stitched in any tucks, resew the border with a normal stitch and remove the basting. This also works great for pieced borders with lots of seams to match.

BORDER OPTIONS

The design will often dictate which of the following options to use.

Butted Borders

Borders with butted corners are the easiest borders to stitch. All the joining seams are straight, with the border seams forming a T where they meet at the corners.

I typically add the side borders first, and then the top and bottom borders. I find this often saves fabric. It's not written in stone, so feel free to swap the order if you wish. If you are following project instructions, be sure to adjust the lengths of the borders accordingly. Refer to Measuring for Borders (page 104) and Stitching Borders (at left) for guidance as needed.

1. Measure your quilt from top to bottom and cut 2 border strips to this length.

2. Fold the quilt in half, top to bottom, to find and mark the midpoint along the sides; repeat for the border strips. Place the quilt top and a border strip right sides together, matching the midpoints; pin.

3. Pin the ends of the border strip to the corners of the quilt top and every 2", easing or stretching slightly to fit. Sew with a ¼" seam and press. Repeat this step for the other side border.

4. Measure your quilt top from side to side, including the borders you just added. Cut 2 border strips to this length. Pin and sew to the top and bottom of the quilt as you did for the side borders; press.

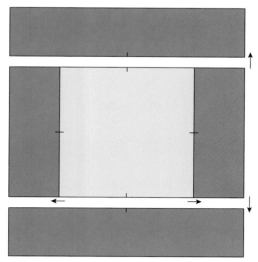

Add the side borders and then the top and bottom borders.

Mitered Borders

Mitered borders have corner seams angled at 45° so that the border truly resembles a picture frame. These borders are a little trickier to sew, but the results are well worth the effort. Refer to Measuring for Borders (page 104) and Stitching Borders (page 106) for guidance as needed.

1. Measure your quilt top from top to bottom. Add 2 times the finished width of the border, plus an extra 2"–3" for "insurance." Cut the side border strips to this length.

2. Measure your quilt from side to side. Add 2 times the finished width of the border, plus an extra 2"–3" for "insurance." Cut the top and bottom border strips to this length.

3. Find and mark the midpoint on each side of the quilt top and on each border strip. From the marked midpoint, measure in both directions and mark half the *length* of the quilt top on each side border. Repeat this step using the *width* of the quilt top to measure and mark the top and bottom border strips.

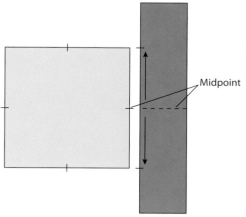

Measure and mark.

4. Place a side border and the quilt top right sides together. Match and pin the midpoints and then the corners of the quilt top with the marked ends of the border strip. The border strip will extend beyond the edges of the quilt top. Use additional pins as needed.

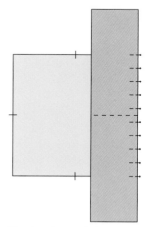

Match points and pin.

5. Stitch the border to the quilt top. Start and end the seam with a backstitch, ¼" in from the corners of the quilt top; press. Repeat for the other side and the top and bottom borders.

Stitch to within ¼" of the corners.

6. Lay a corner of the quilt top right side up on your ironing board. Place a border strip on top of its neighboring border.

7. Fold the top border strip under, so that it forms a 45° angle, and press lightly. Use a ruler with a 45° marking to check that the angle is accurate and that the corner of the quilt is flat and square. Make any necessary adjustments. When you're sure everything is in place, firmly press the fold.

Place one border on top of the other.

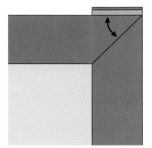

Fold the border strip at a 45° angle.

8. From the corner, fold the quilt top on the diagonal, right sides together, aligning the long raw edges of the neighboring border strips. The fold you've made should form a perfect extension of the diagonal fold in the quilt top. Mark the fold line with a pencil; pin.

9. To sew the miter, backstitch at the inside corner at the point where the border seams meet, and then stitch along the marked fold toward the outside corner of the border. You'll be stitching on the bias, so be careful not to stretch the corner as you sew. Finish with a backstitch.

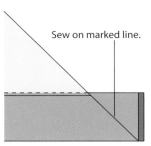

Sew on marked line.

Trim.

Seam

Fold the quilt top to align the fold lines.

Trim.

10. Trim the excess border fabric to a ¼" seam allowance and press the seam open.

11. Repeat Steps 6–10 to miter the remaining corners.

tip

When adding multiple mitered borders, cut all border strips to the length of the outside border. Sew the borders together and stitch them to the quilt as a single unit. You'll only need to miter each corner once.

Partial-Seam Borders

This technique is sometimes used to construct blocks such as Around the Twist. The first border is partially stitched to the quilt and is then finished after the last border is attached. The result is a quirky design twist that I particularly like for striped inner borders. Refer to Measuring for Borders (page 104) and Stitching Borders (page 106) for guidance as needed.

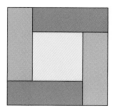

Around the Twist block

1. Measure your quilt top from top to bottom. Add the cut width of the border, minus ½" for seam allowances. Cut the side border strips to this length.

2. Measure your quilt from side to side. Add the cut width of the border, minus ½" for seam allowance. Cut the top and bottom border strips to this length.

3. Find and mark the midpoint on each side of the quilt top.

4. From one end of each side border, measure and mark the *length* of the quilt top. Find and crease the midpoint between the end of the strip and the point you've just marked. Repeat for the top and bottom borders, measuring and marking the *width* of the quilt top and creasing to find the midpoint.

5. Place a side border and the right edge of the quilt top right sides together. Match the midpoints and the bottom right corner of the quilt top with the marked endpoint on the border; pin. (The border strip will extend beyond the quilt's bottom edge.) Align the opposite end of the border strip with the top right corner of the quilt, and pin as needed.

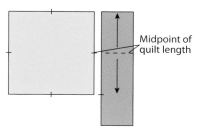

Measure and mark the length of the quilt top and midpoint.

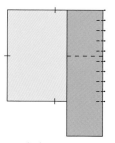

Match the corners and marked points and pin.

6. Stitch the border strip to the quilt top, stopping approximately 3" from the corner of the quilt top; press.

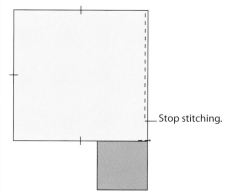

Stop stitching approximately 3" from the corner.

7. Place the top border strip and the top edge of the quilt top right sides together. Match the midpoints and the ends of the border strip with the corners of the quilt. Pin as needed.

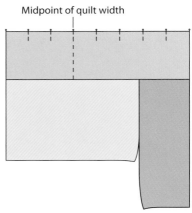

Match marked points and corners and pin the top border.

8. Stitch the border to the quilt; press.

9. Repeat Steps 5–8 to add the left side and the bottom borders.

10. Complete the first border seam; press. If necessary, trim and square the corners of the quilt.

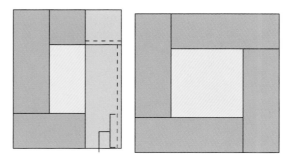

Complete the seam of the first border.

Borders with Corner Squares

Borders with corner squares give a quilt a wonderful, traditional flavor. They are easy to sew and can come to the rescue if you run just a bit short of border fabric.

Cut them from a single fabric or from a variety of fabrics for a scrappy look. If you like, you can even piece them. Just be sure that they relate to the rest of the quilt in color or design. Refer to Measuring for Borders (page 104) and Stitching Borders (page 106) for guidance as needed.

1. Measure your quilt from top to bottom and cut 2 border strips to this length for the side borders. Repeat, but this time measuring your quilt top from side to side for the top and bottom borders.

2. Stitch the side borders to the side of the quilt as described for Butted Borders (page 106).

3. Stitch corner squares onto both ends of the top and bottom border strips; press.

4. Stitch the borders to the top and bottom of the quilt, carefully matching the corner seams; press.

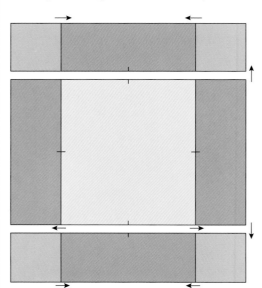

Stitch as shown.

Pieced Borders

A pieced border is a fabulous way to repeat or emphasize a key shape (or shapes) in the body of the quilt.

Whenever possible, plan the finished size of your pieced border unit or block so it divides evenly into the finished measurements of the body of the quilt top. If that's not possible, however, there *are* ways to cope.

One simple solution is to add (or adjust) an inner border to make up the difference. Another is to insert an appropriately sized "spacer" to make the necessary adjustment in the pieced border. This spacer can be a simple strip (aptly called a *coping strip*) or a specially designed unit or block relating to the quilt and border design. Center the spacer in the border or place it randomly. If you wish, use it to change the direction of the border units or blocks.

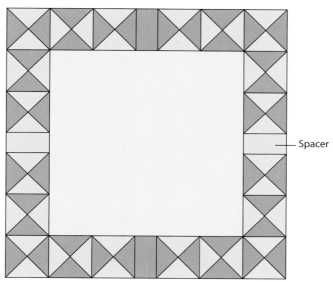

— Spacer

Add spacers to make a border fit.

Turn corners by repeating the border unit or block, substituting (or designing) a special corner unit, or using simple corner squares (see Borders with Corner Squares, page 110).

tip

For a super-simple pieced border, stitch scrappy strips of random lengths together to the desired lengths. This treatment is a great way to use up leftovers, too.

Self-Bordering Quilts

It's possible for a quilt to "create its own border" simply by the way you change the value range of the blocks—or even just the backgrounds of the blocks—ringing the quilt's center, as shown in *Bow Ties*.

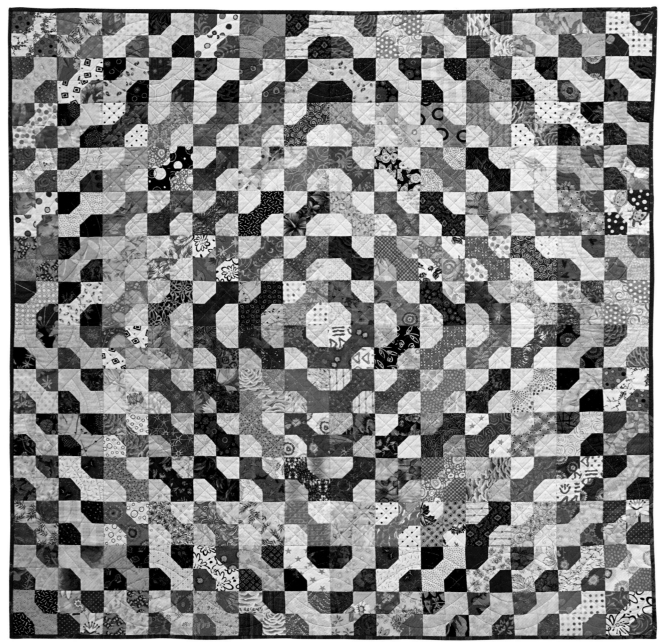

Bow Ties (56½" × 56½")
designed and made by Alex Anderson,
machine quilted by Dianne Schweickert

Scalloped Borders

Scalloped edges give a quilt an elegant, feminine finish. Mark the scallops after you've sewn the borders to the quilt but before basting and quilting.

Sometimes it will be left to you to determine the size of the scallop. In this case, size the scallop so that it divides evenly into the sides and the top and bottom edges of the quilt.

Marking Method 1

1. Divide a side edge of the quilt top into equal sections and mark the divisions. Fold the opposite edge up to the marked side and repeat the markings. Do the same for the top and bottom of the quilt.

2. Decide how deep you want the scallops to be and make registration marks. Trace a plate or something similar to mark the scallops.

3. Baste and quilt as usual, keeping any appliqué or quilting motifs within the marked scallops.

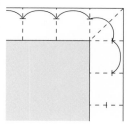

Marking Method 2

At other times, the size of the scallop will be determined by an appliqué or quilting design.

- Option 1: Mark the quilt top, following the curve of the appliquéd scallops, and then baste and quilt as usual.

- Option 2: Baste and quilt a scalloped design. Mark the scalloped edge to follow the curve of the quilting design.

Whig's Defeat
(70″ × 70″)
designed and made
by Linda Jenkins,
machine quilted
by Linda V. Taylor

Appliqué Borders

An appliqué border lends a pleasing touch of contrast to the geometry of a pieced quilt. As always, carry some element from the body of the quilt—color, shape, proportion—into the border so that the design is visually connected. Sometimes you can extend some element of the appliqué over the boundary into the neighboring border or body of the quilt, making the connection even stronger.

Cut and fold lengths of freezer paper to match the border measurements and experiment with full-sized appliqué designs. Or simply cut lengths of bias vine, flowers, leaves, and other pleasing shapes and place the appliqués by eye for a playful free-form look.

tip

It's easier to appliqué the border before it is attached to the quilt top. Appliqué three-quarters of each border, leaving the corners to be finished once the borders are stitched to the quilt.

Blue for Julie
(65" × 80")
designed, made, and
quilted by Jan Magee

CHOOSING AND MARKING YOUR QUILTING DESIGN

You've probably heard the expression "quilting makes the quilt" … and it's true! No matter how complex and accurate the piecing, no matter how lush and intricate the appliqué, until that quilt top is layered and sculpted with thoughtfully selected lines of quilting, a quilt *top* is just that: a flat, two-dimensional expanse of cloth. Add batting and backing, and that surface becomes the canvas for a whole new layer of design, one which—if chosen and executed with care—adds a treat for the eye and an almost irresistible temptation for the fingers to explore.

Of course, good quilting design doesn't just happen. We've all seen examples of *beautifully* designed quilt tops that lose their luster due to poorly conceived quilting. Planning

is essential, and being able to recognize the difference between a successful design that complements and supports and an unsuccessful one that competes or detracts—or, worse yet, just sits there—is essential as well.

Quilting design is a popular topic in my speaking repertoire, and I always start with this compelling question: "Whoever has quilting design down pat, please raise your hand." Never in my years of lecturing has *one person* ever raised his or her hand. This is not to discourage you; instead, it is offered as encouragement. Study every well-considered and well-executed quilt to learn from it and to add ideas for quilting to your tool belt.

WHAT YOU'LL NEED

- Mechanical pencil and eraser
- Black permanent felt-tip pen
- Paper scissors
- Ruler (2˝ × 18˝ clear, see-through)
- Lightbox or light table
- Marking tools
- 1/4˝-wide quilting tape

- **Paper:** Many different types of paper—including individual sheets, pads, and rolls—are available and suitable for designing or tracing quilting patterns. Each has its own benefits and limitations.

  - **17˝ × 22˝ graph paper** (4 or 8 squares per inch)—The light grid lines on this oversized paper make it easy to draw the pattern within the desired space and help keep the pattern evenly spaced when you're dividing up the areas of the quilt to be quilted. If the space you're designing is larger than a single sheet, tape the necessary number of sheets together with clear tape, carefully lining up the grid lines.

  - **Vellum** on a roll—Vellum is a heavy-duty tracing paper that comes on a roll, typically 18˝ or wider. It's translucent, yet strong enough to withstand multiple erasures.

  - **Tracing paper** on a roll—Like vellum, tracing paper is translucent. It's a less-expensive alternative to vellum, but not as durable.

  - **White butcher paper** on a roll—This economical paper is what I use for patterns. It's not translucent, but it's sturdy and can handle multiple erasures.

BASICS OF GOOD QUILTING DESIGN

How do you evaluate what approach is best for *your* quilt? Here are some basic guidelines that will get you off to a good start.

How and by whom will the quilt be used? Is this quilt intended largely for show or to be cherished as a future family heirloom? If so, by all means, pull out the stops and go for your fanciest, most lush quilting. If this is a quilt that the kids are going to drag around or is destined for a bed that the dogs jump on, however, you'll probably want to keep the quilting fairly simple.

Fill the space. Just as you wouldn't want to jam a huge house on a postage-stamp-sized lot, you'll want to make sure that the amount of quilting in your plan is appropriate for the area of the quilt that you're aiming to fill. Not enough quilting, and the space looks awkward and empty, as though you underplanned, became bored, or ran out of time and energy. Too much quilting, and the piece can look cramped; instead of enhancing the space, the quantity of stitching overwhelms it.

The floral motif here is too small for the space.

If you're choosing a quilting motif for a specific area or block, a good rule of thumb is to select a design that comes within ¼" of the seams. If you find a motif that you absolutely love but that's either too large or too small, you can reduce or enlarge it on most copy machines.

Distribute quilting evenly over the entire surface of the quilt. If you fill some areas of your quilt top—for example, the blocks—with heavy quilting and then skimp on other areas, such as sashing or borders, your finished quilt will look unbalanced, be inclined to sag unattractively in the underquilted spots, and pucker where the sparsely and densely quilted areas meet. Think balance.

Uneven amount of quilting

Consistent amount of quilting

Mix curves with geometry and geometry with curves.
There's a reason so many lovely old appliqué quilts feature heavily gridded backgrounds. Those straight lines not only fill in the block backgrounds, but they also make a nice visual counterpoint to the curvy, organic appliqué shapes.

The same holds true for the opposite: gently curved fans, feathers, and cables soften the straight lines and sharp angles of many of our favorite geometric blocks. In other words, embrace the contrast.

Photo by Gregory Case

Grape Escape (50″ × 50″)
designed and made by Alex Anderson
with Pam Vieira-McGinnis,
machine quilted by Paula Reid;
example of appliqué with geometric
background quilting

Angel Quilt
(44" × 53")
designed, made,
and hand quilted
by Alex Anderson,
embroidered by
Estella Gonzales;
example of mostly pieced
quilt with curvy quilting

Don't be afraid to cross the lines. When it comes to quilting designs, seamlines can become arbitrary. Rather than looking at each block as a series of geometric shapes and isolating each shape with quilting, try the "big picture" approach. Consider the whole block as a single design surface. Are there any adjacent shapes that you can highlight with a single quilting motif? What if you were to quilt a wreath or feathered heart over an entire pieced block? Can secondary designs, created where blocks meet, be emphasized by motifs that overlap the block boundaries? It's okay for quilting motifs to cross the lines between blocks and sashing or the quilt center and borders.

Reserve elaborate quilting for areas where it can be seen. If your quilt features especially intricate piecing or areas with highly patterned (busy) fabrics, it's pretty unlikely that your quilting motifs will show to their best advantage. Save those fancy wreaths, feathers, and other elaborate quilting designs for solids, tone-on-tones, and lightly patterned prints, as well as for filling the more open areas on your quilt—such as plain alternate blocks or sashing. That way, every beautiful stitch will be seen. For densely pieced or printed areas, keep it simple.

☐ TROUBLESHOOTING: QUILTING BUSY FABRICS

If your border fabric is so highly patterned that it will disguise elaborate quilting, try one of the following:

- Follow the pattern printed on the fabric with your quilting. This adds texture without adding additional pattern. Just be sure that the density of the quilting remains consistent.

- Try quilting with a thread in a highly contrasting color. Sometimes that's all you need for the quilting to shine.

Quilting with white thread

Follow the pattern on busy fabrics.

- Choose a familiar motif, such as a cable or fan. The repetitive pattern is easily recognized, so the brain fills in the blanks.

Quilting with pink thread

BASIC QUILTING STRATEGIES

The following are some basic quilting strategies:

Stitch in-the-ditch: With this approach, you stitch right next to the seamline on the side of the seam *without the seam allowance*. It's a great way for a beginner to start. Your stitches will be hidden, giving you time to perfect your quilting technique.

¼" or outline quilting: With this method, you stitch ¼" from the sewn seam inside each shape. Many beginning quilters are directed to use this method because it is easy and requires no marking. I typically don't ascribe to this option because it has a tendency to result in an unevenly quilted surface and the seam junctions tend to push forward. Personally, my go-to choice is a crosshatched grid (see the first example at right).

Echo quilting: This method is most commonly paired with appliqué. Begin by stitching right along the outside edge of the appliqué motif, and then again ⅛" to ¼" further outward, using consistently wide bands of stitching, until you reach the outer limits of the block or meet another area of quilting.

An example of echo quilting

Overall grids and designs: These overall patterns cover the entire surface. Overall grids are among my favorites, and the options are endless. You can mark them with your clear, gridded ruler and your favorite marking tool or by using ¼"-wide (or another appropriate-width) masking tape. Here are a few options, from simple to more complex.

An example of ¼" or outline quilting

> **tip**
>
> When you've used tape to mark straight lines for quilting, sew your stitches right next to (not through) the tape.

Other possibilities for overall quilting motifs include fans, clamshells, and circles.

Seeing Stars
(48" × 54")
designed and made
by Alex Anderson,
machine quilted
by Dianne Schweickert

This quilt is intended for love and use, so it is adequately, not overly, quilted. The soft, rolling circles pick up the look of the polka dots in the square blocks. Note that this is also an example of a randomly staggered set (page 98).

OTHER SOURCES FOR QUILTING DESIGNS

Quilting books and magazines often include great ideas for quilting designs; some even include full-sized patterns for you to trace. You'll also find an amazing and varied selection of clear plastic templates (or stencils) available at your local quilt shop or via your favorite quilting mail-order or Internet source, to use for blocks, sashing, and borders.

Digital cameras have made it easy to record quilting inspiration when you're out and about. Keep your eyes peeled for interesting architectural details and tilework, unusual textures in nature, and unique patterns in wallpaper or decorating fabric. Once you start looking, you'll find design inspiration everywhere! Just be careful that you are not infringing on anyone's copyright.

TROUBLESHOOTING: ADAPTING DESIGNS FOR MACHINE QUILTING

If you're planning to quilt by hand, pretty much anything goes. For machine quilting, however, there are a few simple guidelines to consider.

Many traditional quilting patterns and stencils are noncontinuous motifs. That means they involve numerous "overs and unders" (or broken lines) that require you to make frequent stops and starts in your stitching, which is a fussy and time-consuming process.

Lots of these patterns can be easily adapted for machine quilting. Study a pattern to see if it is possible to connect the breaks and still maintain a good sense of design. The cable below is a good example. The version on the left is a traditional, noncontinuous cable. But by connecting the "overs and unders," you can make the quilting lines continuous and turn it into an easy motif for machine quilting.

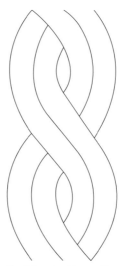

Traditional cable motif

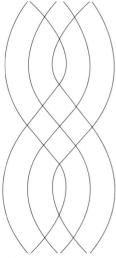

Cable adapted for continuous-line machine quilting

IDEAS FOR CREATING YOUR OWN MOTIFS

The following techniques are fun and yield many options for creative quilting design.

Eight-Section Designs

1. Cut a paper square the size of the area you need (¼" smaller than the pieced area to allow for seam allowances).

2. Fold in half vertically and horizontally.

Fold in half.   Fold in half again.

3. Fold in half diagonally, and then draw and cut an arc on the large end of the shape.

Fold in half diagonally.   Draw and cut an arc.

Twelve-Section Designs

1. Cut a paper square the size of the area you need (¼" smaller than the pieced area to allow for seam allowances).

2. Fold in half vertically and horizontally.

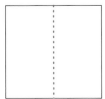

Fold in half.   Fold in half again.

3. Fold in thirds to create 3 triangle shapes.

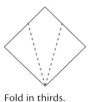

Fold in thirds.

4. Draw and cut an arc on the large end of the shape.

Draw and cut an arc.

Options:

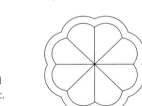

Optional eight-section design

Another eight-section design

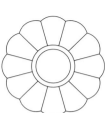

Optional twelve-section design

Another twelve-section design

As your confidence builds, you'll discover how easy it is to create your own designs. There is a plethora of commercial templates available. With a copy machine, it's easy to increase or decrease the size to fill the space.

Soft, Curved Lines

Picture an organic shape and how it flows softly from one unit to another. Hold that image in your mind as you try this approach.

1. Divide your quilt top into 2 sections: the center and the border. For the center, draw a few lines across the surface of the quilt. Have them flow gracefully from either the edge of the quilt center or from each other. Keep the curves open and flowing and larger than 90°.

2. Draw echo-quilting lines about 1" apart, using the main curving lines as your guide. (This is an excellent pattern for machine quilting. An example of echo-quilting lines can be seen in *Angel Quilt*, page 118).

3. When you're satisfied with the center, consider using a geometric grid in the border. The two styles (organic and geometric) work well together.

Geometric grid in border

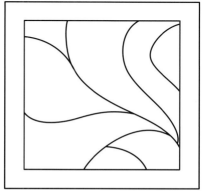
Draw soft curved lines.

Draw echo-quilting lines.

TRANSFERRING THE DESIGN

Once you've decided on a quilting plan, it's time to transfer the motifs to your quilt top. Quilting templates are easy. Just place the template *on top of* the area you wish to mark and trace the design with your preferred marking tool, connecting the broken lines in the stencil as needed. When you use premade plastic templates, you can mark either before or after you baste the quilt.

If you're transferring a design that you've drawn yourself or traced from a book or magazine, position the pattern *underneath* the area of the quilt top you wish to fill. If you're working on light fabric, you should be able to see through the fabric easily. If not or if you're working with a darker fabric, re-mark the paper pattern with a black permanent, felt-tip marker, and then transfer the design, section by section if necessary, with the aid of a lightbox or light table (page 17).

Never use a graphite pencil to mark quilting designs; the markings may not come out.

tip

When using a water-soluble pen, try not to mark too long before you intend to start quilting. Also, once your quilt is marked, don't expose it to heat, direct sunlight, or the iron, all of which can make the marking difficult to remove later. *Always test the marking tool to make sure it will come off.*

STRAIGHT-LINE QUILTING

Straight-line quilting includes any quilting that is—surprise!—stitched in straight lines. This includes anchoring (see Anchoring, page 148) and other ditch quilting, outline quilting geometric shapes within blocks and borders, and quilting single or parallel straight or diagonal lines and grids. Doubling the lines adds incredible texture to the finished quilt.

Solace (13" × 18") designed, made, and machine quilted by Alex Anderson

STIPPLE QUILTING

Sometimes called meandering or meander quilting, stipple quilting is a popular choice for machine quilting. It follows no pattern, but wanders, or meanders, over the quilt surface in a maze of curving lines. It works beautifully as filler behind appliqué motifs and stands equally well on its own. The curves resemble the interlocking edges of jigsaw pieces; in traditional stippling, the curving lines never cross. Most quilters do not mark stippled designs, but quilt them freeform instead.

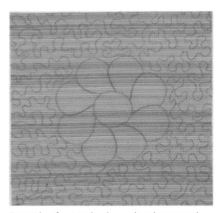

Example of properly planned and executed stipple quilting

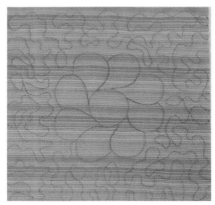

Example of poorly executed stipple quilting; lines should never cross.

Choosing a quilting strategy is not an exact science. There is no *one* perfect answer. The possibilities are endless, and inspiration is all around you. Now that you have some good, solid guidelines in your quilter's tool belt, the foundation is in place. It's simply a matter of auditioning and experimenting until you find just the right match for your quilt.

> **tip**
>
> Stitching behind a motif such as a flower or cable causes unstitched areas to pop forward, increasing their importance in the design. It also adds a luxurious layer of texture to the quilt. Be sure to keep a balance in the size of the motif and the scale of the background quilting, so the primary motif doesn't pooch.

Motif with no background quilting

Motif with gridded background

PREPARING TO QUILT

As with most other endeavors, taking the time to carefully and thoroughly prepare your quilt top for quilting goes a long way toward ensuring a successful outcome.

HOUSEKEEPING

In preparation for basting, carefully press the finished quilt top. Begin by pressing from the back of the quilt, making sure that there are no "flop overs" (that is, seam allowances that change directions midseam). Trim loose threads to prevent them from shadowing through, and then turn the quilt over and press it from the front to make sure there are no tucks.

CHOOSING AND PREPARING A BATTING

Your batting should be 2"–4" larger than your quilt top on all sides, including stretcher strips for hand quilting (see Basting for Hand Quilting in a Hoop, page 130).

Cotton: Most older quilts are filled with 100% cotton batting. Although it can be more difficult to hand quilt than polyester, wool, or silk, cotton re-creates that antique appearance, and it drapes beautifully. It's also a natural fiber, which allows the quilt to breathe.

Cotton batting should be heavily quilted, with lines of quilting spaced no more than 1"–2" apart to prevent the batting from shifting, pulling apart, and becoming lumpy over time, particularly when the quilt is washed.

I recommend 100% cotton batting (or at least 80% cotton content) for machine quilting. The cotton fabric in the quilt top and backing clings to the cotton in the batting, which greatly reduces shifting in the layers as you quilt. Cotton is also sturdy and stands up to the rigors of the machine-quilting process. (Polyester can be stretchy.)

Some cotton battings must be prewashed, so be sure to read the manufacturer's instructions for any required pretreatment. (That said, it's a good idea to check the packaging for guidance before using *any* batting product.)

Polyester: Nowadays, polyester batting comes in a range of lofts, from low to extra high. Low loft is wonderful for a densely pieced quilt (all those seam allowances!) or to replicate the soft, drapey look of cotton batt. It's also a great choice for beginners or for quilts you plan to tie. Medium loft is just a little thicker, adding more body and additional warmth.

With polyester, you don't need to quilt as heavily as with cotton; every 2"–3" is fine. Some of the newer varieties even allow you to space your quilting as much as every 6".

Cotton/polyester blend: The mix in blended battings is typically 80% cotton and 20% polyester. It has many of the advantages of cotton batting but is easier to quilt through, with minimal bearding. This type of batting requires lines of quilting no more than 3" apart. Some require prewashing; so again, check the packaging for guidance.

Wool and silk: Although these alternatives can be expensive, there is nothing as wonderful as quilting on a wool or silk batting. Your needle will slide through like butter, and—as with cotton—wool and silk are natural fibers that allow the quilt to breathe.

Bearding occurs when the fibers from the batting migrate through the quilt top, creating little tails of fuzz on the surface. This can be a real issue, particularly when your quilt top contains lots of dark-colored fabrics. In that case, opt for a batting made from cotton or a cotton/poly blend, rather than polyester. Polyester, a synthetic fiber, is super strong, and the migrating bits tend to linger on the surface of the quilt. Natural cotton fibers are more likely to break at the surface.

CHOOSING AND PREPARING THE BACKING

Plan on a backing that is about 2"–4" larger than your quilt top on all sides, including stretcher strips for hand quilting (see Basting for Hand Quilting in a Hoop, page 130). This allows for shifting and shrinkage of the layers that may occur during the quilting process. (For a tied quilt, 2" extra on all sides should be enough.) Don't use a sheet or a piece of decorator fabric for the backing when hand quilting—these are too thick and difficult to needle through!

If your quilt top includes lots of light fabrics, choose a light fabric for the backing so it doesn't show through to the front.

> **tip**
>
> If you plan to have your quilt quilted by a longarm professional, check in advance to determine his or her batting and backing requirements.

> **tip**
>
> The day before you plan to use it in your quilt sandwich, remove the batting from its packaging. Unroll it and spread it out on a bed or on the floor (away from pets or curious little ones), so that wrinkles and folds can begin to relax. Don't forget to launder it if the manufacturer recommends prewashing.

Piecing the Backing

If your quilt is larger than 42" wide, you'll need to piece the backing.

1. Trim the selvages before piecing backing sections together.

2. Divide the backing fabric across its width into 2 (or 3) equal pieces.

3. Sew the pieces together along their long, lengthwise edges, with a ½" seam.

4. Press the seams open to distribute the bulk.

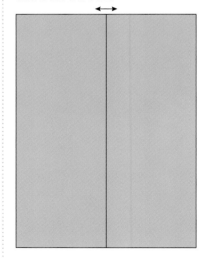

Of course, you could also piece the backing just for fun, incorporating leftover fabrics or blocks from the front of the quilt.

BASTING

Basting holds the layers together and prevents them from shifting during quilting. The basting will be removed when the quilting is finished.

As many experienced quilters will tell you, this not the place to skimp! Shortcomings at the basting stage will only multiply as you move on through the quilting process. The care you put into the basting will bear strongly on the final outcome of your quilting efforts.

I most often baste my quilts by spreading the layers flat on the floor. Think of this process as quilting yoga. You may be a little stiff in the morning, but the results—a beautifully flat and square quilt—are worth the effort.

1. Press the backing and spread it, right side down, on the floor or another clean, flat surface. (If you have carpet, make sure that it is nonloop.) Stretch the backing taut but not tight and affix the edges to the floor every 2″ or so with T-pins (for carpet) or masking tape (for bare flooring).

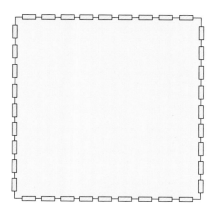

2. Gently lay the prepared batting over the backing.

3. Center the quilt top, right side up, over the prepared batting and backing.

4. Use a large ruler to straighten and square the quilt, beginning with the outer border. Use the straightened outer-border seam as a guide for straightening any long vertical and horizontal seams in the quilt's interior.

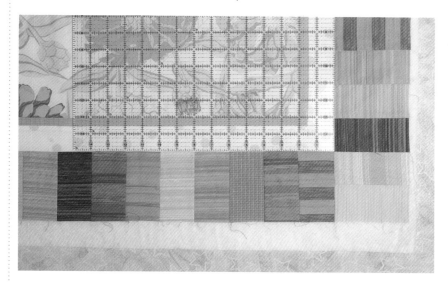

tip

If you aren't able or prefer not to baste on the floor, you can use a large tabletop instead. You probably don't want to do this on your dining room table—the needle or pins may scratch—but there are alternatives. Be sure that whatever surface you choose is clean and smooth and that you can raise or lower it (or your chair) to spare your back.

A Ping-Pong table with the net removed makes a great basting space.

Check with your church, library, or quilt shop; all may have large tables that you can push together to use as a single large surface and probably have the space for you to do so. Again, make sure the table (or your chair) can be modified for the sake of your back.

Basting for Hand Quilting in a Hoop

Stitch a "stretcher" strip of fabric, approximately 6″ wide, to all sides of the quilt top before basting. This allows you to maintain the proper hoop tension as you quilt all the way out to the borders of your quilt and helps keep the edges of your quilt from stretching.

Using a long thread and a large needle, take large stitches through all three layers. Don't bother knotting the other end of the thread as you finish each line of basting stitches. When it's time to remove the basting you can just give the knotted end of the thread a little tug and it will pull out.

I like to baste in a grid pattern (about every 4″), so there is an even amount of basting throughout the quilt.

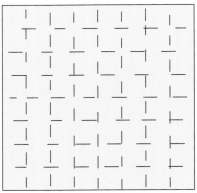

Baste in a grid.

> **tip**
>
> Use the bowl of a spoon to pick up the tip of the needle as it comes through all the layers.

> **tip**
>
> Use light-colored thread for basting, as the dye from darker thread might migrate onto the fabric and leave spots when the basting is removed.

Basting for Machine Quilting

Use safety pins (see Pins, page 16) for basting. You can remove them easily as you come to them. You don't need anything fancy (such as bent pins); just avoid anything too large. Rustproof size #1 pins are a good choice. The colored ones are extremely pliable, easy to see … and fun!

1. Working in quadrants from the center out, secure the 3 layers (top, batting, and backing) together with safety pins placed every 3″. Try not to place pins where you will quilt over them. Pin baste all the way to the edges of the quilt, but don't close the pins yet.

2. Release the quilt sandwich from the floor. Working carefully with the quilt in your lap, close the safety pins.

> **tip**
>
> To save time, I use a basting spray such as 505 Spray and Fix Temporary Fabric Adhesive (see Resources, page 174) in lieu of safety pins for basting small quilts that I plan to machine quilt. If you choose this option, be sure to check the needle periodically for product residue.

READY, SET, ... QUILT!

Now it's time to consider how you're going to quilt the top by machine or hand. Or is tying your quilt (page 154) the best solution? Your ultimate decision will be determined by the look you want to achieve and/or the intended final use (or user!) of the quilt.

WHAT YOU'LL NEED

- **Needles:** Quilting needles (betweens)—I recommend that you start with a size 8, then try a size 9, and so on. Some quilters swear by a size 12 (the smallest size), but personally, I can't thread them, and they're too fragile for me. I use a size 10.

- **Thread:** Quilting thread— I generally use quilting thread, as it is a bit stronger than sewing thread. But feel free to experiment and play.

- **Thimble (page 132)**

- **Hoop or frame:** I recommend a 16″ or 18″ quilting hoop. Do not use an embroidery hoop; it's too small and lightweight and will not hold the desired tension. As you become captivated with the process of hand quilting, you may want to invest in or build a frame.

HAND QUILTING

I've always enjoyed the hand-quilting process and find that hand-quilted quilts have a special look, feel, and drape.

Placing the Quilt in a Hoop

> **note**
> To avoid puckers, quilt from the center of the quilt to its outer edges.

When you're quilting in a hoop, the key is to keep the tension in the quilt sandwich taut but not tight. Loosen the screw of the hoop and separate the rings. Slide the smaller ring under the center of your basted quilt, and place the larger hoop (with the screw) on top of the quilt. Making sure that the top and the backing are smooth and equally stretched, clamp the rings together and partially tighten the screw.

Press your hand down in the middle of the hooped area, while continuing to keep the layers equally stretched. This will loosen the tension just enough so that you can more easily manipulate the needle while quilting.

Remove the hoop from your quilt between quilting sessions to avoid any stretching and distortion that may occur by leaving the quilt in the hoop for an extended period of time.

Selecting a Thimble

A thimble is a must if you're going to execute the proper quilting stitch. At first, wearing a thimble may seem awkward, but you'll be amazed at how quickly you'll adapt.

Make sure that the thimble has a nice fit. It should be comfortable, but not so loose that it falls off when you shake your hand gently.

After you've determined whether you prefer to wear your thimble on your middle finger, pointer finger, or thumb (pages 134–140), consider investing in one of the beautiful thimbles available on the market today. You—and your quilts—deserve this treat!

Classic metal thimble, with indentations on both the sides and the end

Open-ended thimble, with a ridge at the end so that the needle won't slide off under your fingernail

Ridge-tipped thimble—perfect for working off the end of the thimble

The Quilting (Rocking) Stitch

Although it may *look* just like a simple running stitch, the quilting stitch is unlike any other sewing stitch. This unique stitch is called the rocking stitch and is created using a rocking motion while the thimble pushes the needle through all three layers of the quilt. This motion requires three important fingers on your two hands working in unison. On the top of the quilt (using your dominant hand, or the hand you write with), you will use your thimble finger and thumb. Under the quilt, you will use either the pointer finger or middle finger of your other hand. All three fingers work together to manipulate the needle through the hills and valleys that your fingers create.

You'll need to identify the finger you want to wear the thimble on. I wear the thimble on my pointer finger. Many quilters prefer their middle finger. Either is fine. Try both to see which one feels the most comfortable.

Your next decision is whether you plan to use the end or the side of the thimble to push the needle. This will determine what type of thimble you'll need (see Selecting a Thimble, at left). I find that most middle-finger quilters use the end of the thimble, while pointer-finger quilters (like me) prefer to work off the side. Again, experiment to see what works best for you.

Your early stitches will most likely feel a bit awkward at first. Stick with it! With a little practice and patience, the rocking stitch will become second nature—kind of like riding a bike.

tip

To keep your stitches less visible, match the thread color as closely as possible to the color of the fabrics you are quilting on. This is a good strategy for beginners; however, as you become more confident with your stitches, you might envision your quilting as a more visible design element. In that case, try thread in a contrasting color. (Oh ... and it's okay to use more than one color of thread in your quilt.)

Preparing to Stitch

Thread has a wrap, just like a rope. Threading your needle while the thread is still on the spool keeps the wrap of the thread going in the right direction. This results in less tangling.

Thread the needle with a single strand of thread, no longer than 18". Once the needle is threaded, snip the thread free of the spool. Make a knot at the end of the snipped thread.

The Quilter's Knot

This is a very simple knot that is wonderful for many sewing situations. Easy to master and easy to hide.

1. Hold the threaded needle in 1 hand and the tail in the other. Make a circle with the thread at the end closest to the spool, crossing the top thread over the bottom thread. Pinch it together with your forefinger and thumb.

2. Slip the needle under the circle and come up through the circle.

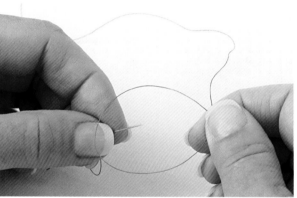

For lefties

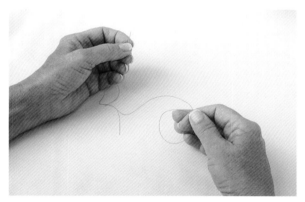

For lefties

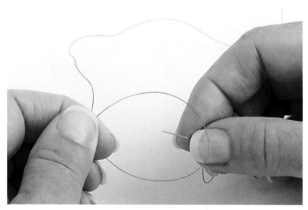

For righties

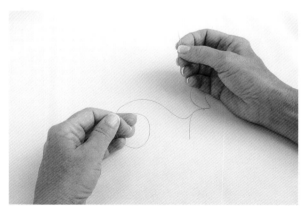

For righties

3. Pull both tails of the circle to make the knot.

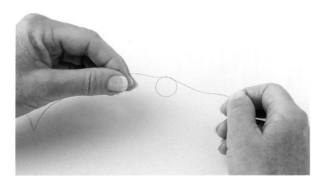

For lefties

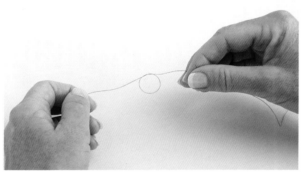

For righties

4. Insert the threaded needle into the quilt top and batting (not the backing) an inch away from the point at which you want to start quilting. Bring the needle up at the spot you plan to start stitching. Gently tug the thread until the knot "pops" in between the layers. This is called *burying the knot*.

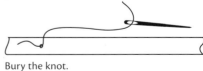

Bury the knot.

5. Put the hand without the thimble under the quilt, positioning your pointer or middle finger—whichever is more comfortable—where you will be taking the first stitch.

Thimble on Middle Finger

1. Place the hand with the thimble on top of the quilt. Hold the needle straight up and down between the thumb and ring finger. With the hand in the "C" position, insert the needle straight down into the quilt where the hill has been created by your finger underneath.

For lefties

For righties

2. Release your fingers from the needle.

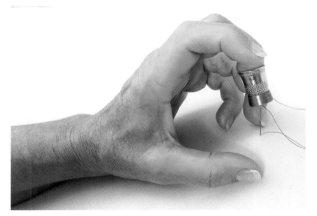

For lefties

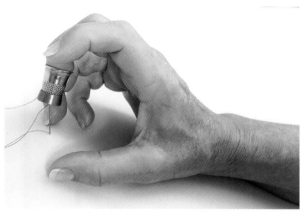

For righties

3. When you feel the prick of the needle on your finger below the fabric, you'll do 2 things at once. Using a dimple of the thimble to control the needle, pivot the needle tip back up through the layers. At the same time, press down with your thumb in front of the hill where the stitch is about to be made. (The needle should now be flat against the quilt.) This forces the tip of the needle through the top of the hill, creating the first stitch.

For lefties

For righties

4. As soon as you see the tip of the needle come through the hill, move the finger that is under the quilt away. Pivot the blunt end of the needle back up so that it is perpendicular to the quilt, forcing the tip down into the valley. This needle motion is about a 90° movement. As soon as you feel the tip of the needle lightly prick your finger under the quilt, repeat the process, gathering 2 or 3 stitches at a time on to your needle. Then pull on the needle and thread to draw the thread taut and complete the stitches.

tip

With experience, you'll be able to get more than two or three stitches on the needle, but try not to load more than half your needle. If you do, the needle might get stuck in the quilt, slowing down the entire process. You'll also want to limit yourself to two or three stitches per needle when your stitching motifs involve lots of curves, such as feathers or grapes.

Thimble on Pointer Finger

1. Place the hand with the thimble on top of the quilt. Hold the needle straight up and down between your thumb and middle finger. With your hand in the "C" position, insert the needle straight down into the quilt where the hill has been created by your finger underneath.

For lefties

For righties

For lefties

For righties

2. Release your fingers from the needle.

For lefties

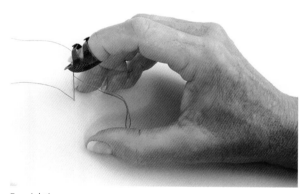

For righties

3. When you feel the prick of the needle on your finger below the fabric, you'll do 2 things at once. Using a dimple on the thimble to control the needle, pivot the needle tip back up through the layers. At the same time, press down with your thumb in front of the hill where the stitch is about to be made. (The needle should now be flat against the quilt.) This forces the tip of the needle through the top of the hill, creating the first stitch.

For lefties

For righties

4. As soon as you see the tip of the needle come through the hill, move the finger that is under the quilt away. Pivot the blunt end of the needle back up so that it is perpendicular to the quilt, forcing the tip down into the valley. This needle motion is about a 90° movement. As soon as you feel the tip of the needle lightly prick your finger under the quilt, repeat the process, gathering 2 or 3 stitches at a time on to your needle. Then pull on the needle and thread to draw the thread taut and complete the stitches.

For lefties

For righties

Thimble on Thumb

Sometimes, particularly if you're quilting in a frame, you'll want to stitch away from yourself. To do this, you'll need to control the needle with your thumb, rather than your pointer or middle finger.

Many people prefer this method because the thumb is a much stronger finger. The result is faster stitching. Also, if your hand tires, it's nice to get relief by stitching in another direction. As an added bonus, you'll find quilting feathers and grapes a snap.

You'll need a larger thimble that fits comfortably on your thumb. You will use the side of the thimble to control the needle, not the end. At first, it might seem a bit awkward to handle the needle with a thimble on your thumb, but you'll be amazed at how quickly you get used to it.

1. Hold the needle straight up and down between the thimble finger and your pointer and middle fingers. Insert the needle into the quilt top straight up and down, lightly pricking your finger underneath.

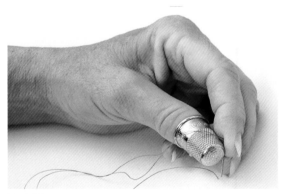

For lefties

For righties

2. As soon as you feel the tip of the needle prick the underneath finger, roll the thimble to the top of the needle.

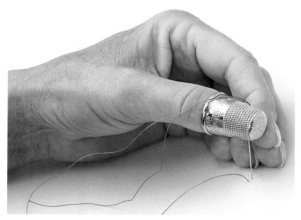

For lefties

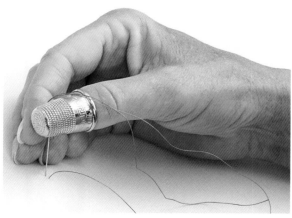

For righties

3. Rock the blunt end back, forcing the needle parallel to the quilt. With the pointer finger on your top hand, push down in front of the hill, where you'll be taking the first stitch. Keep your hand in the "C" position.

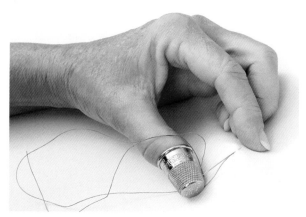

For lefties

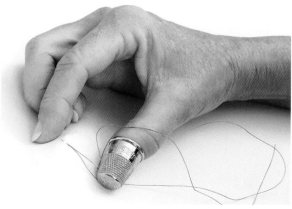

For righties

4. As soon as you see the tip of the needle come through the hill, move the finger that is under the quilt away. Pivot the blunt end of the needle back up so that it is perpendicular to the quilt, forcing the tip down into the valley. This needle motion is about a 90° movement. As soon as you feel the tip of the needle lightly prick your finger under the quilt, repeat the process.

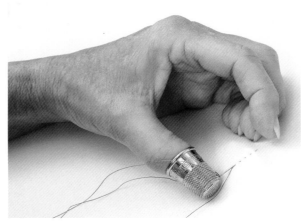

For lefties

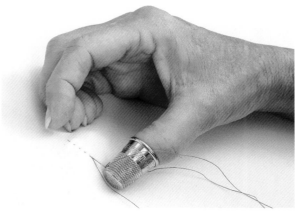

For righties

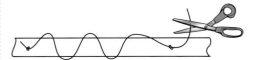

tip

If your needle gets sticky with oxidation from sweaty fingers or humidity or if it gets bent or dull from use, throw it away.

Finishing and Burying the Knot

As you come to the end of the thread, tie a knot close to the quilt surface. Put the needle into the same hole from which it emerged and then back through the quilt top. Pull gently on the thread, burying the knot between the layers. (Some quilters like to take a little backstitch for extra insurance.) Pull up the remaining tail of thread and carefully trim the end.

To secure your stitches, it's important to bury the knot at the beginning and ending of your hand quilting.

■ Don't worry about the size of your stitches; focus instead on consistent stitch length. Counting the stitches on top, my first stitches were two to the inch!

■ The smaller the "hill," the smaller your stitches will be.

■ Don't pick out poor stitches as you go. This takes away from valuable learning time. When the quilt is finished, you can always go back and replace those early stitches, but my guess is, it won't be worth your time. In fact, you may not even be able to find them!

■ You don't need to tie off the thread to move from one section of your quilt design to another. If the distance you need to travel is smaller than two needle lengths, consider "walking the needle." In the direction you want to travel, insert the needle halfway into the quilt top, between the top and the backing. Bring the tip of the needle halfway up through the top of the quilt. Grab the tip of the needle and pivot the eye, which is still between the layers. Leading with the eye of the needle, push the needle back down into the quilt, continuing in the desired direction. When you get to the intended destination, push the needle up through the top surface of the quilt and continue stitching.

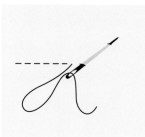

Insert the needle between layers.

Pivot the needle between layers and push the eye of the needle through.

■ If your first stitch is always larger than the rest, try tilting the needle forward just a bit, rather than inserting it straight up and down. Another option is to take a backstitch to "cheat" the look.

Tilt the needle forward slightly.

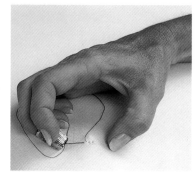

Take a backstitch.

Machine Quilting

Welcome to the wonderful world of machine quilting! You're about to begin an exciting journey that will add a whole new dimension to your quilting life.

WHAT YOU'LL NEED

- **Thread:** The sky is the limit when it comes to thread (see Thread, page 15). However, if you've been dialed into machine quilting at all, you've probably heard reference to monofilament. Monofilament is used when you want the machine quilting to be virtually invisible on the surface of the quilt. It comes in clear and in a smoky gray color that disappears into darker fabrics.

Clear and smoky monofilament thread

Monofilament can be either nylon or polyester. I highly recommend that you stick with the polyester product. Nylon can stretch or become brittle with age. Be wary of products labeled polyamide. Although this sounds like polyester, it is a nylon product and is not best suited to your quilting needs.

- **Needles:** Probably the most important consideration is that your needle and thread are compatible. If you make this match using a higher-end needle and good-quality thread, you're halfway home.

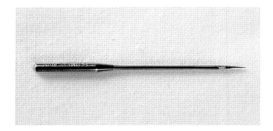

Machine needles have sizes; the higher the number, the larger the needle (that is, the wider the shaft).

Needles marketed as machine-quilting needles have a special taper (and thicker groove) that narrows down to a slightly rounded point. A size 90/14 is a good choice to start with. As you improve, you may wish to move to a smaller, finer needle. A finer needle makes smaller holes, and the stitching appears more precise.

Choose a needle with a wide enough eye that it doesn't shred the thread. For this reason, some quilters (myself included) prefer a topstitch needle, which has a large eye and a deeper groove, making it a good choice for use with metallic and decorative threads.

- **Specialty feet:** You'll want a walking foot attachment for straight-line quilting (see Feet, page 11). I prefer an open toe, so you can see where you're going. You'll also want an open- or closed-toe darning foot for free-motion quilting (see Free-Motion Quilting, page 152). These attachments are shown in the feet photos (page 11).

- **Gloves and other goodies:** Many tools are available to help with the free-motion quilting process. All are designed to give you a better grip and more control on the quilt sandwich as you stitch, thus improving your ergonomics and easing the tension in your hands and shoulders. These tools include specially made gloves, foam paddles, "stick-um" for your hands, and finger cots. Note that these tools are *not* generally intended for use with the walking foot, where the feed dogs, rather than you, move the quilt sandwich.

Samples of helpful notions for free-motion quilting

■ TROUBLESHOOTING FOR NEEDLES

If …

> You've been sewing for 6–8 hours, or
> You're beginning a new project, or
> You hear a dull or "punching" sound when the needle goes through the fabric

Then …

> Change to a fresh needle.

If …

> Your thread shreds

Then …

> The eye of the needle is probably too small. Change to a needle with a larger eye (a topstitch needle, for example).

If …

> You're removing the needles from their packaging and need to remember which is which

Then …

> Label the sections of a tomato pincushion and use it for easy storage and identification.

If …

> You have used needles to dispose of and are concerned about safety

Then …

> Use an ice pick (carefully!) to make holes in the top of an empty pill container and drop the spent needles inside.

Adjusting the Tension

As you get ready to machine quilt, you'll want to make sure the tension on your sewing machine is set correctly. Ideally, you want *just a speck* of bobbin thread to show on the top of your quilt and *just a speck* of top thread to show on the back. If you see anything more, your tension needs to be adjusted.

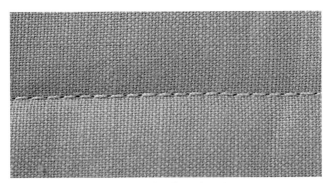

Example of stitching with properly adjusted tension

If you can see more than a speck of bobbin thread on the front of your quilt, you need to *loosen* the top tension; that is, change the setting to a *lower* number. More than a speck of top thread showing on the back of the quilt is a sign that you need to *tighten* the top tension, or change the setting to a *higher* number.

It's always a good idea to make a small sample quilt sandwich using the fabric and batting you plan to use in your quilt. Practice machine quilting on the sample using the needle and thread(s) you plan to use for your project. Adjust the tension on your machine as needed. Begin at your machine's normal or automatic tension setting, and then make slight adjustments as needed, testing as you go. When you've found the proper setting, make note of the materials and tension setting in a small notebook that you keep just for this purpose. If you record the specifics, you'll have them on hand if your work on the project gets interrupted for an extended period of time—for example, by other sewing tasks. The settings will also be available for future projects using similar materials.

Handling Bulk

One of the challenges eventually faced by all machine quilters is how to handle the bulk of the quilt at the sewing machine. The larger the quilt, the more bulk you'll need to manage.

You can use any one of many techniques to bundle or package your quilt. Experiment a bit to find the one that suits you best. You may find it easier to keep your initial efforts on the small size. Once you feel confident handling these smaller projects under the needle, you'll be ready to move on to larger quilts.

I like to quilt my quilts from the center out, half at a time, to make sure I don't quilt any bubbles (or mountains!) into the center. This strategy also ensures that I never have more than half of the quilt between the needle and the machine. I also find that quilting from the center out makes it easier to manipulate the quilt, which tends to become stiffer and less pliable as it is quilted.

1. Spread your quilt out flat. Roll or scrunch the right edge of the quilt evenly toward the center, stopping a few inches from where you intend to place the first line of quilting.

2. If necessary, either roll or accordion-pleat the left side of the quilt as well. If the table surface is large or the quilt small enough, you may be able to simply arrange the left edge of the quilt on the surface. Be sure the weight of the quilt is distributed evenly.

3. Take the quilt to your sewing machine. Outfit your machine with the proper foot (see Feet, page 11), needle (page 142), and thread, top and bottom (see Thread, page 15, and Machine Quilting, What You'll Need, page 142). Make sure that the presser foot is raised and the needle is in its highest position. Position the quilt so that the rolled or pleated edge is under the arm, the area you've left free is under the needle, and the rolled, pleated, or otherwise-arranged left edge is supported on your work surface to the left of the machine.

Right side of the quilt is rolled.

tip

Here's a good rule of thumb for choosing which thread weight and color to use: If you want your stitches to show dramatically, use a heavier thread (#40 or #30) in a contrasting color. If you want your stitches to blend into the background, use a finer thread (#60 or #70) in a matching color. Just remember to change the needle according to the thread weight.

Sample stitched with medium #50 thread in a slightly contrasting color

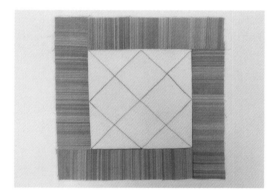

Sample stitched with heavier variegated #40 thread

Sample stitched with finer matching #60 thread

Starting and Stopping

Now it's time to sit down at your machine and get started.

Starting

1. Reduce your stitch length down almost (but not exactly) to 0 and lower the presser foot right over the spot where you plan to start quilting. Holding onto the top thread, take a complete stitch, so that the needle returns to its highest position.

2. Without raising the presser foot, gently tug the top thread to pull the loop of bobbin thread to the quilt surface. Pull the bobbin thread through to the top.

Take a complete stitch, ending with the needle at its highest position.

Pull the top thread to bring the loop of bobbin thread to the surface.

3. Insert the needle into the exact spot where the bobbin thread came up. Drop the feed dogs, if desired, and hold the threads to the side as you take 1 or 2 stitches.

Insert needle and take 1 or 2 stitches.

4. Gradually increase the stitches to the full stitch length (approximately 10–12 stitches per inch) within 6–8 stitches. You're on your way!

Stopping

The process of stopping reverses the process you used for starting. As you get within six to eight stitches of a planned stopping point, gradually decrease the stitch length. Drop down almost (but not exactly) to 0 and take one or two stitches. Lift the presser foot and gently pull the quilt away from the machine. Cut both the top and the bobbin thread, leaving a nice long tail on each.

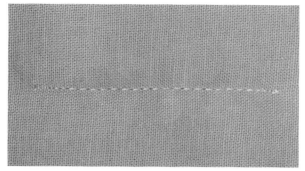

Transition the length of your stitches to begin and end your quilting.

Dealing with Thread Tails

There are two basic options for coping with the thread tails at the starting and stopping points of your machine quilting. My preference for eliminating thread tails is to pull the tail away from the quilt and use small sharp embroidery scissors or thread clippers *to slice*—not clip—the thread as closely as possible to the quilt surface. The tiny stitches you took at the starting and stopping points secure the threads. By slicing in a sideways and slightly upward motion, you avoid the possibility of accidentally cutting into the quilt.

Slice, don't clip, the thread tails.

tip

Some machine quilters prefer to tie off and bury the thread tails. If you haven't already done so, pull the bobbin thread to the top by gently tugging on the top thread. Thread the tails onto a hand-quilting needle and make a knot close to the surface of the quilt. Insert the needle into the top two layers of the sandwich, right at the point where the stitching begins or ends. Run the needle between the layers for an inch or two, bring it back to the surface, and give it a gentle tug until you hear the knot "pop" between the layers. Trim the remaining tail as described in Dealing with Thread Tails (at left).

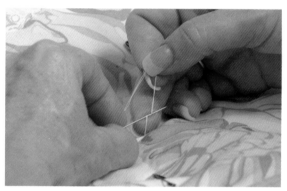

Make a knot close to the surface of the quilt.

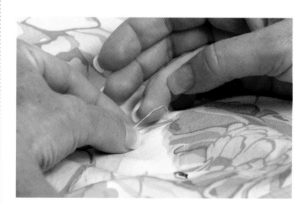

Pull the needle through the layers to bury the knot.

Whichever method you choose, you can do your cleanup each time you stop, or you can wait until you have finished an entire section before going back for cleanup. If you choose the latter, be careful not to catch the tails in your subsequent stitching.

Anchoring

Before you begin quilting any motifs or background filler, anchor the key seams in your quilt—those seams between the rows of blocks, sashing, and borders. It's important to get as close to the seam as possible. Be careful, because the pressed seam allowance can jump from one side to the other between the blocks and sashing in the long seams, and you want your anchoring to be as straight and invisible as possible. This is called stitching in-the-ditch (see Basic Quilting Strategies, page 120).

Stitch in-the-ditch.

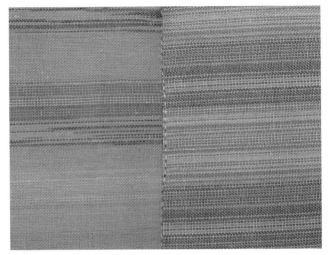

An example of poorly executed stitching in-the-ditch

An example of properly done, well-hidden stitching in-the-ditch

This stitch supplements the basting and helps keep the layers secure as you add the more decorative stitching.

1. Outfit your machine with the walking foot attachment. Begin at one edge and stitch the centermost long vertical (or diagonal) seam. Next, quilt all vertical seams (or diagonals) to the right of this center line. Rotate the quilt from top to bottom, roll the other side of the quilt to fit under the arm, and quilt the vertical (or diagonal) lines on the other side of the center line.

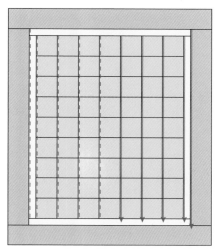

Stitch, beginning at the centermost seam.

2. Rotate your quilt, roll it where necessary, and quilt the centermost horizontal (or opposite diagonal) long seam of the quilt. Quilt first to one side of the center line and then to the other side, as you did in Step 1.

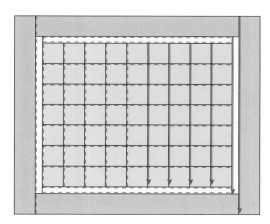

Remember to sew as close to the seam as you can, stitching along the side of the seam that is free of pressed seam allowance.

tip

To camouflage your anchoring stitches, match the thread color to the quilt top.

◼ TROUBLESHOOTING FOR STOPS, STARTS, AND TENSION

If …

The thread clumps or snarls when you take the first few machine-quilting stitches

Then …

You may have forgotten to hold the top and bottom threads while taking the first few stitches, or

You may have set your starting stitch length too low. You want to set it almost—but not quite—to 0.

If …

You see more than just a speck of bobbin thread on the top of your quilt or top thread on the quilt back

Then …

The tension on your machine needs adjustment (see Adjusting the Tension, page 144).

If …

Your quilt is being puckered or pulled as you stitch

Then …

Stop stitching!

The quilt may be hung up under your chair or on the corner of the table, or

The thread may be catching underneath the quilt, in which case you'll want to stop, tie off, and check the bobbin before proceeding.

Machine-Quilting Technique

Just as with hand quilting, stitch consistency is a primary goal for machine quilting. There is one way to get there: master the fundamentals and practice, practice, practice!

I make it a practice to warm up before beginning (or resuming) any session of machine quilting. It puts both my body and my mind in the right place. I encourage you to do this, too.

Make yourself a small practice sandwich, using muslin for the quilt top and the same batting and backing as you will use in your quilt. This sandwich can double as the vehicle for testing and adjusting the machine tension (see Adjusting the Tension, page 144). Remember: You can't jump from project to project and assume the settings will stay the same. Fabric, batting, needle, and thread all affect the tension setting.

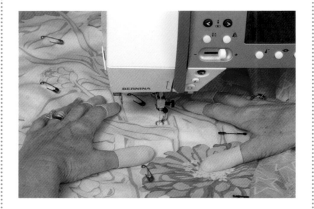

tip

Position your hands on the quilt sandwich to maximize the area you can stitch before you'll need to reposition them, but not so far apart that you are uncomfortable or lose control of the quilt top.

One of the biggest mistakes new machine quilters make is trying to go *too fast*. Just because you are quilting by machine doesn't mean you must finish the quilt "yesterday." Keep the pace slow and methodical—you are sewing, not riding Seabiscuit! Machine quilting can be a repetitive, meditative activity—probably slower in pace than you might think—so relax and enjoy it.

This next tip will be a tough one, but train yourself *not* to look at the needle as you stitch. Look an inch or so ahead of the needle to anticipate where you are going, rather then where you are or have already been. This prepares you to react, keeping you both relaxed and in control … and— I promise—the needle *will* go up and down!

When you need to stop and reposition either the quilt sandwich or your hands, always stop and restart in the exact same needle hole. This is where both the knee lift and the needle up/needle down functions will prove extremely helpful. When you foresee an adjustment, try to make the transition in an area where the thread color matches the fabric, so the transition will be invisible.

Finally, be kind to your body. Occasionally pause, raise your head, and gaze softly into the distance to relax your eyes. Stop for a stretch every 20 minutes or so. Gently move your head in small circles and ear to shoulder. Raise and lower your shoulders to keep them loose. If you are feeling especially tense, take a more extended break. Go for a walk, work in the garden, have a cup of tea. You'll come back to the sewing machine feeling refreshed and ready to go again.

Straight-Line and Simple-Curve Quilting

Straight lines can be tricky. (Have you ever tried to draw a straight line without a ruler?) Many machine quilters use a walking or even-feed foot attachment, with feed dogs up, for straight-line quilting. These attachments guide the multiple layers of fabric through the machine evenly, minimizing the chance for shifting and puckers. In the beginning, you'll want to use your walking foot for straight-line quilting. Once you have mastered free-motion quilting, however, you may find that you prefer to do your straight-line quilting that way (see Free-Motion Quilting, page 152) as well, to avoid turning the quilt to change direction.

As with all machine quilting, take it slowly when straight-line quilting. Don't pull on the quilt; let the foot and the feed dogs do most of the work. For large areas, quilt parallel lines, grids, and other crosshatched designs using the top-to-bottom, side-to-side strategy described for anchoring (page 148). It may seem tedious to end each line of stitching at the bottom and then begin anew at the top, but this will allow you to stitch large sections without turning the quilt—an advantage you will come to appreciate quickly!

Many simple curves (see Soft, Curved Lines, page 125) can also be machine quilted using the walking foot with the feed dogs up. These gentle curves make a nice substitute for grids and other overall straight-line designs on the surface of a strongly geometric pieced quilt.

Example of straight-line quilting

Some walking foot/even-feed attachments, particularly the newer ones, come with a built-in guide that rides the previous line of stitching and helps you stitch subsequent lines that are parallel and evenly spaced. If you have one of these attachments, you may find you can skip marking, particularly for smaller areas, such as block backgrounds or borders. (Personally, I prefer to mark.)

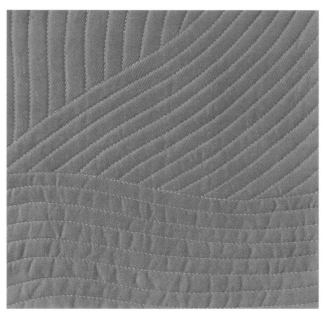

Example of gentle curve quilting

While the walking foot is on your machine, you might want to try this fun technique that many modern quilters are enjoying today: pick a familiar stitch or one of the fancy, decorative stitches on your machine and experiment to customize it as you wish.

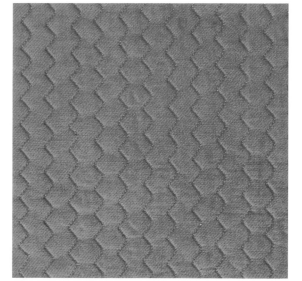

Play with the stitches on your machine. The options are endless!

Free-Motion Quilting

Free-motion quilting is the best method for quilting cables and wreaths, stipple quilting, echo quilting around appliqués, and other patterns that require lots of curves and changes of direction. With free-motion quilting, you—rather than the machine—move the fabric under the needle and guide the direction of the stitching *without having to turn the quilt.* Most quilters accomplish this by using a darning foot attachment and dropping the feed dogs on the machine. Others—myself included—have had success leaving the feed dogs up, depending upon how tight the curves and how complex the motif. I encourage you to try both ways to see which method you prefer.

On one thing most quilters agree, use the darning foot (see Feet, page 11) for free-motion stitching. There are basically two types of darning feet to consider as you begin your machine-quilting journey: open toe and closed toe. I prefer the open over the closed toe because it allows me to have greater visibility as I stitch; however, the closed toe will work just fine.

Example of free-motion quilting; this is a great warm-up exercise for even the seasoned quilter.

If your machine has a slide control button, slow it down! Machine quilting isn't a horse race!

Start stitching to get the feel and motion of the process. Doodle, just like you did when you were a kid. Try your hand at meandering. Then, how about a chain of small flowers? Finish with your signature—after all, this is your first thread painting!

■ I learned this trick from noted machine quilter Sue Nickels, and it's become my favorite: Find a pair of dishwashing gloves that fit snugly. (The dollar or variety store is a good source.) Cut off the fingers and place a finger from the glove on your thumb, pointer, and middle finger of each hand. Instant control! You'll see this trick in action in Machine-Quilting Technique, Tip (page 150).

■ Following the fabric motif (see Troubleshooting: Quilting Busy Fabrics, page 119) is a super-easy way to practice free-motion quilting. It requires no marking, and slight wobbles or variations in the stitching will be hidden in the fabric print. It's also a wonderful way to experiment with different types and colors of threads.

Stipple Quilting

Practice drawing stipple designs on paper first so you can become accustomed to the movement of the design. Study your drawings to determine a starting and ending strategy. It's okay to start off the quilt top or bump out to the edge again if you find yourself caught in the stippling maze.

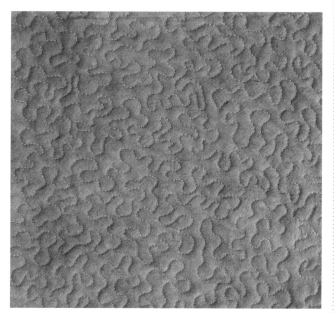

Example of stipple quilting

PRACTICE, PRACTICE, PRACTICE

Make yourself a small practice sandwich, using muslin for the quilt top and the same batting and backing as you will use in your quilt.

Turn on some good music—whatever helps you relax or takes you to a spot that makes you happy. This is a wonderful way to aid the transition out of your linear left brain and into your creative right brain.

Begin by quilting some straight lines and then some doodles, such as curlicues and stars. Try writing your name. As you begin to loosen up, experiment by "drawing" one of the motifs you intend to quilt. This will give you confidence, as well as the opportunity to test your stitching strategy. I always do a prominent motif planned for the quilt as part of my practice exercise.

Sample warm-up exercise

■ TROUBLESHOOTING FOR QUILTING

If …

Your machine is skipping stitches

Then …

Your needle may be dull, burred, or bent; time for a change, or

The pressure on your presser foot may need adjustment. Check your machine manual for guidance.

If …

You're getting tucks or pleats in the back of the quilt

Then …

You may not have basted properly or sufficiently. Remove the quilt from the machine, return to your basting surface, and adjust as needed, or

You may need to change to the walking foot attachment on your sewing machine.

If …

You feel like the sewing machine or the quilt is "driving" you, rather than vice versa

Then …

Stop, take a deep breath, and slow down. You're probably going too fast.

TYING YOUR QUILT

Sometimes tying, rather than quilting, your quilt is the best solution. (Think quilts for kids, charity quilts, etc.) You'll tie your quilt after basting but before binding. As for batting, polyester is your best bet.

Perle cotton, embroidery floss, yarn, or even super-thin ribbon work really well for tying. You'll also need an extra-long needle with an eye large enough to thread the floss, yarn, or ribbon.

1. Thread a large needle with the tying thread.

2. Insert the needle from the top through to the back of the quilt. Reinsert the needle from the back so that it comes through to the front about ¼" from the original point of entry.

3. Pull the thread until you have a thread tail about 3" long remaining on top of the quilt.

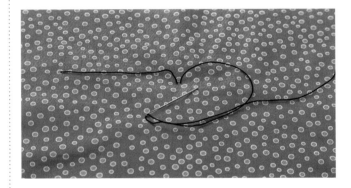

4. Trim the long end of the thread to leave a tail about 3" long.

5. Tie a square knot and then tie a second square knot.

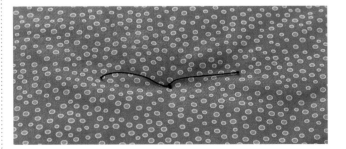

6. Trim the thread tails so they are about 1½"–2" long.

FINISHING TOUCHES

The purpose of any edge-finishing treatment is to enclose and protect the raw edges of a quilt's three layers. Depending upon how you'll use your finished quilt, the edges can receive lots of wear and tear. This is one reason I don't recommend turning the backing to the front to create a self-binding.

In addition to being functional, finishing is also a design decision. The treatment you select for your quilt is your final chance to make a statement, so make your choice carefully.

WHAT YOU'LL NEED

- Sewing machine
- Rotary cutter
- Rotary mat
- Rotary ruler
- Pins
- Thread
- Marking tools
- Iron and pressing station

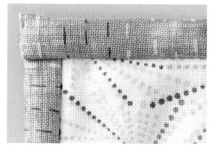

Binding with squared corners (page 158)

Binding with mitered corners (page 159)

Binding a zigzag edge (page 160)

Binding a scalloped edge (page 161)

Faced edge (page 163)

Folded flat piping (page 165)

Prairie points (page 166)

BINDING

The most common method of finishing a quilt is with an applied binding, which goes on *after the quilt is quilted*. Making your own binding gives you unlimited choices in color and fabric and guarantees that the quality of the binding fabric matches the rest of the quilt. Use your design wall to experiment with various fabrics and to get a sense for how wide you want the finished binding to be.

There are several ways to make and apply binding. The best choice for your quilt will depend upon the quilt's size, intended use, and design. Equip your machine with a walking foot (or engage the even-feed feature, if your sewing machine has one) for smoothly applied, pucker-free binding.

Straight-Grain vs. Bias Binding

Binding strips can be cut on either the straight grain or the bias of the fabric (see Fabric Grain, page 18).

Binding cut on the straight grain—preferably crosswise—is my choice for finishing quilts with straight edges.

Binding cut from the *crosswise* grain has a bit of stretch. Although it may require piecing to get the desired length, it often requires less fabric, and—since strips cut crosswise are often slightly off-grain—it minimizes the chance that any one single thread runs the entire folded edge of the binding, which would make it more vulnerable to wear.

Binding cut on the true diagonal—or *bias*—of the fabric is excellent for finishing curved edges. Because it has a fair amount of stretch, bias binding eases comfortably around curves. In addition, binding cut on the bias tends to wear better, since it is cut across, rather than along, the weave.

Because it tends to stretch, take extra care with bias binding. Handle it gently and use lots of pins to avoid getting ripples in the finished edge.

Detail of striped bias-cut binding on straight-edged quilt

Detail of striped bias-cut binding on quilt with softly curved edges

Figuring Binding Length

To figure how much binding you'll need for a quilt with straight edges, measure around the outside edges of your quilt top, and then add *at least* 16″ for seams, starting and finishing, and turning corners.

To figure how much binding you'll need for a quilt with curved (for example, scalloped) edges (see Binding a Scalloped Edge, page 161), run a length of string around the outside edges and add at least 12″ for seams, starting, and finishing.

When you need to piece strips to get the necessary length of binding, piece them with diagonal seams (see Cutting and Grainline, page 104). Press seams open to prevent lumps in the binding, and match thread color to the binding fabric to keep seams less noticeable.

tip

Add an interesting design element to your quilt by piecing the binding from a variety of different fabrics you've used in the top. If you use strips of random lengths, you won't need to worry about a seam falling in an awkward spot. Just trim the length of the troublesome strip—no math!

Example of pieced binding

Double-Fold Binding

Double-fold binding, also called French-fold binding, is what I use for my quilts. The double thickness makes it extra sturdy—perfect for a quilt destined for lots of use. You can double-fold both straight-grain and bias binding.

To figure how wide to cut the binding strips, multiply the desired finished width of the binding by 4. Add ½″ for the seam allowance and an additional ⅛″ to turn over the edge of the batting. So for a crisp, narrow (⅜″-wide) double-fold binding, cut the binding strips 2⅛″ wide (⅜″ × 4 = 1½″ + ½″ = 2″ + ⅛″ = 2⅛″).

1. Figure the length of the binding you need for your quilt (see Figuring Binding Length, at left). Piece the strips end to end with diagonal seams (see Cutting and Grainline, page 104).

2. Fold and press lengthwise, right sides out.

tip

Store binding on an empty paper-towel roll to keep it neat and tangle free until you need it.

Preparing the Quilt for Binding

The binding on your quilt should be firm; that is, the batting should extend to fill it completely. This looks better and is better for the life of the binding.

1. Use your rotary cutter to trim the batting and backing even with the raw edges of your quilt top, to straighten the sides, and to square the corners of your quilt. Take care not to trim off any important block elements (such as points).

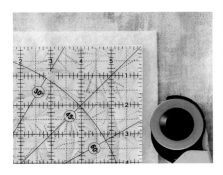

2. Machine baste with a large stitch around the perimeter of the quilt top, approximately ⅛"–³⁄₁₆" inside the raw edge. This secures the 3 layers as you sew the binding to the quilt.

Binding with Squared Corners

Adding individual binding strips separately to each side of your quilt is the easiest of all binding treatments. The binding ends are neatly squared, so you don't need to worry about turning corners.

1. Prepare the quilt for binding by trimming the backing and batting (see Preparing the Quilt for Binding, at left.)

2. Measure the quilt from top to bottom (see Measuring for Borders, page 104). Cut, fold, and press lengthwise 2 binding strips the length of the quilt plus 1".

3. Working from the front of the quilt, center and align the raw edges of the binding strips with the raw edges of one side (left or right) of the quilt top, allowing the strip to extend ½" past each corner. Sew the strip to the quilt with a ¼" seam. Repeat this step for the opposite side of the quilt.

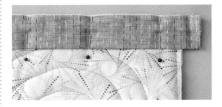

4. Bring the folded edge of the binding over the raw edges to the quilt back, covering the seamline. Use matching colored thread and small stitches to slipstitch the binding securely to the quilt back. Trim the ends of the binding even with the quilt.

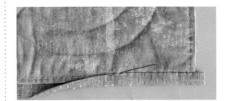

5. Measure the quilt from side to side, including the binding. Cut 2 binding strips the width of the quilt plus 1". Fold and press lengthwise, turning under the 2 ends by ½" to create a finished edge.

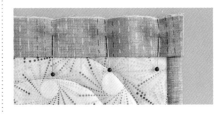

6. Align the raw edges of a binding strip with the raw edges of the top and bottom of the quilt top and the turned-under ends with the corners of the quilt. Sew the binding to the quilt.

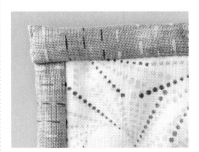

7. Bring the folded edge of the binding to the quilt back, pin, and slipstitch in place. Stitch the ends closed.

Binding with Mitered Corners

Binding with mitered corners is my personal favorite. Miters aren't difficult, and I like the polished look they give. Two methods for finishing the ends are given here. In both cases, you'll start by measuring and preparing the quilt for binding.

Mitered Binding with Tucked Ends

1. Open and trim the starting end of the binding at a 45° angle and press under a ¼″ seam allowance. Refold the binding.

2. Beginning at least 12″ from a corner, align the raw edge of the binding with the raw edge of the quilt top. Pin up to the first corner.

3. Leave the first few inches of binding free and stitch the binding to the quilt with a ¼″ seam. Stop and backstitch ¼″ from the first corner.

4. Lift the presser foot and needle, and rotate the quilt a quarter turn to the left. Fold the binding strip so it forms a 45° angle and extends straight above the quilt, its raw edge even with the raw edge of the quilt top.

5. Fold the binding strip straight down, aligning its raw edge with the edge of the quilt top. Resume stitching at the folded edge.

6. Continue pinning and stitching the binding to the quilt, turning each corner as described in Steps 3–5. As you approach the starting point, stop and trim the end of the binding so it overlaps the start by about 3″.

7. Tuck the remaining end of the binding inside the folded end, making sure the join is smooth. Pin and finish stitching the binding to the quilt.

8. Bring the folded edge of the binding over the raw edges to the quilt back, covering the seamline. Use matching-colored thread and small stitches to slipstitch the binding securely to the quilt back. A miter will form naturally at each corner. Stitch both the front and back miter closed with an invisible (blind) stitch.

Mitered Binding with Seamed Ends

This method of binding finishes with a seam, rather than by tucking one end inside the other. The join is less obvious since there is less bulk.

1. Prepare the quilt and binding as usual. Do not angle or turn under the end of the binding. Sew the binding to the quilt, stopping approximately 10″–15″ from where you started stitching the binding to the quilt. Take the quilt from the machine to a flat surface, such as your ironing board or cutting mat.

2. Lay the tail end of the binding strip over the unstitched starting tail, aligning the raw edges of both strips with the quilt top. Crease the ending tail, or mark it with a pencil, at the point where it meets the start. Measure the *cut* width of the binding strip from the crease (or pencil mark). Cut the ending tail at this point.

3. Open both tails and place them right sides together at a 90° angle. Mark a diagonal seam, pin, and stitch with matching thread.

4. Trim the excess binding to a ¼″ seam allowance and press the seam open. Refold the binding strip and finish stitching it to the quilt.

Binding a Zigzag Edge

If you decide to finish your quilt with a zigzag or stair-step edge, you'll need to miter inside, as well as outside, corners. Cut individual strips and piece them together end to end with diagonal seams (see Cutting and Grainline, page 104). Use the seamed-end method (see Mitered Binding with Seamed Ends, at left) for joining the starting and ending tails of the binding.

1. Mark the desired zigzag edge on the quilt top. Staystitch ¼″ from the trimmed raw edges all around the perimeter of the quilt sandwich.

2. Cut on the marked lines through all 3 layers of the quilt sandwich, and then clip into each inner V just a hair short of the stitching line.

3. Working from the front of the quilt, and not starting at either an inner V or an outer corner, pin and stitch the binding to the quilt with a ¼" seam. Treat the outer corners just as you would a typical mitered binding (see Binding with Mitered Corners, page 159).

4. As you reach an inner V, pull the edge of the sandwich to form a straight edge; stitch.

5. Press the miter into place on the front side of the quilt.

6. Turn the binding over the edge of the quilt. Secure the binding to the backing with matching-colored thread and small invisible stitches. If you wish, finish by stitching the miters closed.

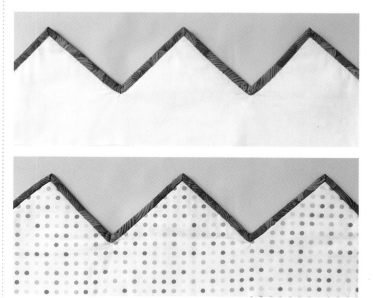

Binding a Scalloped Edge

For this treatment, you'll need binding strips cut from the bias of the binding fabric. Cut individual strips and piece them together end to end with diagonal seams (see Cutting and Grainline, page 104). Use the seamed-end method (see Mitered Binding with Seamed Ends, page 160) for joining the starting and ending tails of the binding.

1. Machine baste a scant ¼" inside the marked scallop. Trim the layers along the marked scallop line.

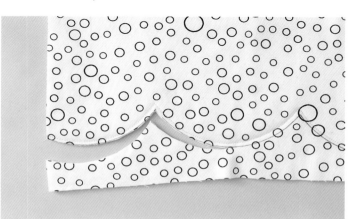

2. Make a mark ¼" inside each V on the front side of the quilt sandwich. Clip the raw edge at each V, stopping just before the mark and basting stitches.

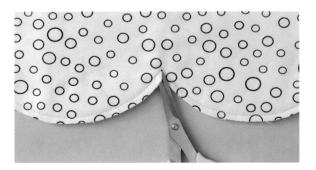

3. Working from the front, begin pinning the binding to the quilt, aligning the raw edge of the binding to the raw edge of the quilt top. Start on the side of a scallop, rather than on the center of a scallop or in a dent, and place the pins perpendicular to the edge of the quilt for easy removal. Gently ease the binding around the curve, taking care not to stretch the binding in the process.

4. At the first V, spread the scallop to form a straight line. Continue pinning the binding to this "straight" edge, placing a pin on either side of the dent to keep the binding aligned. Continue your way around the quilt, pinning the binding to each scallop and dent.

5. Working from the back, stitch the binding to the quilt with a ¼" seam. Remove each pin as you reach it. Stitch each V just as you pinned it—by gently separating the scallops to sew a straight seam. Make sure to stay inside the clip.

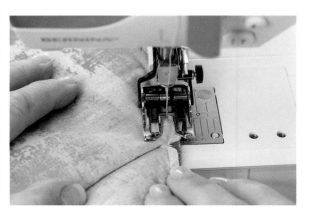

6. Beginning along the side of a scallop and working a scallop at a time, turn the binding over the raw edge of the quilt and use matching-colored thread and small invisible stitches to secure the binding to the quilt back. Stop just before you reach the first V.

7. Make a fold and carefully coax the binding to the back of the quilt. Cover the seamline, match the fold to the point of the dent to form a miter, and continue stitching.

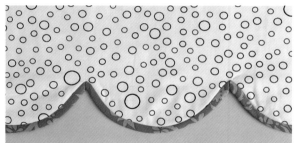

FACED EDGE WITH HANGING SLEEVE

A faced edging is a great finish for your more arty pieces or for those instances where you prefer not to add an additional design element with binding. The design races out to the edges of the quilt, with no added fabric to disturb the design, and the topstitching that completes this method yields an edge that is razor sharp. The method I describe here even includes a built-in hanging sleeve! To keep it nice and flat, use a slat, rather than a round rod or dowel, to hang a faced quilt.

1. Measure the quilt from top to bottom (see Measuring for Borders, page 104). Cut 2 facing strips 3″ wide × the length of your quilt.

2. With right sides together, align the raw edges of the strips with the raw edges of the left and right edge of the quilt top; pin.

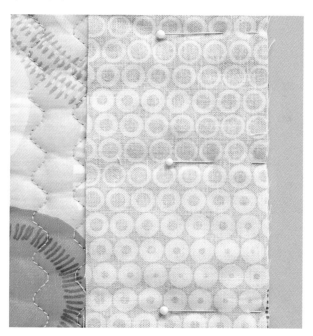

3. Sew the strips to the quilt with a ¼″ seam. Press the strips away from the quilt and topstitch ⅛″ from the seam through all layers.

4. Fold the strips on each side to the back of the quilt, pressing as you go to roll a *tiny* edge of the quilt top to the back as well; pin.

5. Turn under ¼″ on the long raw edge of each facing strip, press, and hem with matching thread and small invisible stitches.

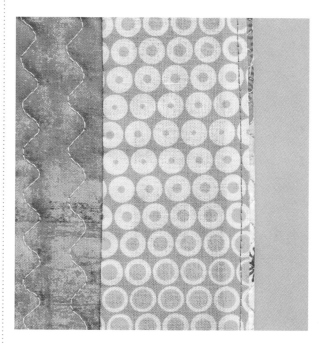

6. Measure the quilt from side to side. Cut a 3″-wide strip equal to this measurement plus 1″. With right sides together and raw edges aligned, center and pin the strip to the bottom of the quilt. The strip should extend about 1″ beyond the quilt at both ends.

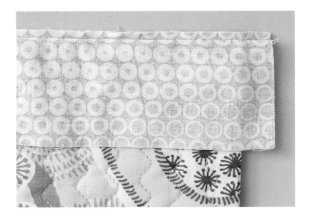

7. Repeat Steps 3–5 to attach, press, topstitch, and hem the bottom strip, neatly tucking in and closing the excess strip at each end with matching thread and small invisible stitches.

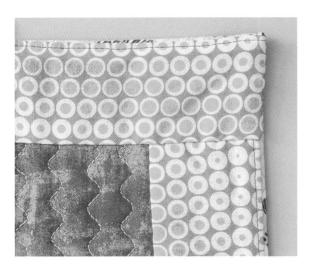

8. Cut a 5″-wide strip equal to the width of the quilt plus 2″. With right sides together and raw edges aligned, center and pin the strip to the top edge of the quilt. The strip should extend 1″ beyond the quilt at both ends. Repeat Steps 3 and 4 to attach, press, and topstitch the top strip in place. Fold back the excess strip at both ends to create a finished edge; press.

9. Turn under a ¼″ on the long raw edge of the facing strip, press, and hem with matching-colored thread and small invisible stitches. Leave the ends open; the top facing will now double as a hanging sleeve.

FOLDED (FLAT) PIPING

A folded, flat, narrow piping acts like a double mat on a framed picture, adding a flash of color and a touch of elegance. To figure how wide to cut the piping, multiply the desired finished width of the piping by 2, and add ½″ for seam allowances.

> **tip**
>
> For quilts with straight edges, cut strips from the straight grain of the fabric. For quilts with curved edges, cut strips on the bias.

1. Prepare the quilt and binding as usual. Measure the quilt from top to bottom and from side to side (see Measuring for Borders, page 104). Add 2″–3″ to both measurements. Cut and prepare 2 piping strips, each to these measurements.

2. Pin the piping strips to the appropriate sides of the front of the quilt, aligning the raw edges with the raw edges of the quilt top. The strips should overlap and extend beyond each corner by 1″–1½″. Baste the strips to the quilt with a ⅛″ seam.

3. Align the raw edges of the binding with the raw edges of the piping and quilt top. Stitch the binding to the quilt using your chosen technique. Trim the excess ends of the piping strips.

4. Turn and stitch the binding to the quilt back with matching-colored thread and small invisible stitches.

PRAIRIE POINTS

Prairie points are overlapping triangles made from folded fabric, adding dimension to the edges of your quilt. They can be cut from a single fabric or from two or three different fabrics, or they can be totally scrappy.

Unlike bindings, which cover the outside edges of the quilt, prairie points are inserted *between the layers*; that is, they are sewn to the quilt top before it is layered and quilted.

Keep the size of the prairie points in proportion to the rest of the quilt. If you're unsure what size to use, cut, fold, and audition points of various sizes.

tip

The long, raw edge of the prairie point equals the side of the cut square. Since prairie points overlap, you'll need extra to cover the measurements of the quilt.

1. Fold each square on the diagonal, right sides out; press. Then, fold in half along the folded side; press.

2. Fold the quilt top in half in both directions and crease to find the midpoint on each side.

3. With right sides together and raw edges aligned, place prairie points along one side of the quilt top. Center a prairie point over the midpoint first, and then place one at each end, making sure the openings of all the prairie points face the same way.

4. Fill the side with additional prairie points. Slip the folded edge of each unit inside the open end of its neighbor, overlapping as needed to evenly fill the space. (You can use elements in the quilt top as guides for spacing.) When you are satisfied, secure each point with a pin placed perpendicular to the raw edge.

5. Repeat Steps 3 and 4 for the remaining sides of the quilt top, making sure to match the number of points on opposite sides.

6. Sew the prairie points to the quilt with a ¼" seam, pivoting at the corners and removing pins as you go.

7. Layer, baste, and quilt the quilt, stopping approximately ½" from the edge and moving the prairie points out of the way as necessary.

8. Trim the backing ¼" beyond the raw edges of the quilt top and prairie points. Carefully trim *only the batting* slightly less than the raw edge of the quilt top and prairie points.

9. Turn (or press) the prairie points away from the center of the quilt, allowing the seam allowance to turn inward. Wrap the backing over the edge of the batting. Secure the backing to the prairie points with pins or basting, and then hand stitch with matching-colored thread and small invisible stitches.

10. If desired, finish with a line of quilting ¼" from the folded edge, all around the perimeter of the quilt.

ADDING A HANGING SLEEVE

At some point, you may wish to display your quilt on the wall. If you plan to enter your quilt in a show, be sure to carefully read the rules regarding the size and application required for the sleeve.

1. Cut a strip of fabric the width of the quilt × 8″ wide. Hem each of the short edges.

2. Fold the strip in half lengthwise, wrong sides together, and stitch. Press the seam open.

3. Position the sleeve with the long seam against the back of the quilt. Pin and whipstitch the long folded edges to the back of the quilt.

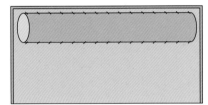

tip

With this method, the sleeve is attached to the quilt before the binding (page 156) is added.

1. Cut a strip of fabric the width of the quilt × 8″ wide. Hem each of the short edges.

2. Fold the strip in half lengthwise, wrong sides together, aligning the long raw edges.

3. Center and align the long raw edges of the sleeve with the top edge of the quilt back; machine baste using a scant ¼″.

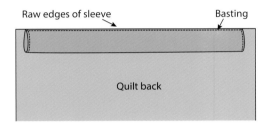

Raw edges of sleeve   Basting

Quilt back

4. Apply the binding as usual. The stitching that secures the binding to the top edge of the quilt will also secure the top edge of the sleeve.

5. Pin and whipstitch the bottom edge of the sleeve to the back of the quilt.

MAKING A LABEL

The information that you include on your label will be treasured for generations to come. Use a permanent fabric pen on the back (or even the front, if the design lends itself) of the quilt, or create a beautiful patch designed especially for the quilt with hand or machine embroidery, colorful fabric pens, or fonts and photos that you print on your computer.

For assurance that the identifying information will not be lost (and to deter theft), some machine quilters attach the label to the quilt backing before basting so that the label is permanently affixed by the quilting. Another option is to write identifying information directly on the quilt where the label will cover it, ensuring that the info will remain even if the label itself is lost or removed.

The following information should be considered essential:

- The name of the quilt
- Your name and the name of the quilter (if different)
- Where and when the quilt was made
- You may also like to add the dimensions of the quilt— handy when you are entering the quilt in a show.

If the quilt is made for a special person or occasion, you might like to add the following:

- The name of the recipient (if the quilt is made to celebrate the birth of a child, add the child's birth date and place, the parents' names, and your relationship to the child)
- The special occasion for the quilt (such as birth, christening, graduation, wedding)
- Any additional personal sentiments

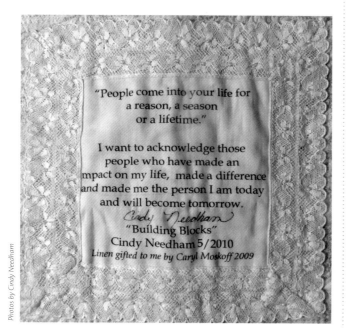

Photos by Cindy Needham

Special labels created by Cindy Needham

■ CARING FOR YOUR QUILTS

If you have a top-loading washing machine, here's what I recommend for washing your quilts:

1. Fill the basin in your washing machine with cool water and mix in a mild soap. (If you're concerned about fabric bleeding, see Troubleshooting: Triage for Bleeding Fabric, page 30).

2. Place the quilt in the washing machine and allow it to soak, occasionally swishing the quilt around in the water with gentle hands. *Do not* use the agitate cycle on the washing machine.

3. Allow the quilt to soak for approximately 20 minutes. Advance to the rinse cycle and give the quilt a cool-water rinse; then run a gentle spin cycle to remove the excess water.

4. Remove the quilt from the machine and air dry it flat, face down on a large light-colored towel or sheet. If it's a nice day, dry it outdoors in a spot where birds are not likely to visit.

tip

If you don't have a top-loading machine or if your machine won't allow you to prefill before adding the quilt, launder your quilt the old-fashioned way by soaking it in the bathtub instead. Drain the water and press the quilt gently against the side of the tub to remove excess water (and weight!) before removing the quilt to dry.

Dry cleaning a quilt is always a risky business. If a quilt is made of materials that cannot be washed, and it's hopelessly filthy, you *might* want to risk it. Be aware, however, that it *is* a risk (including the possibility that the colors might run) … every time!

As for storing your quilts, the best way is unfolded on a bed—layered, if you like—and covered with a sheet to protect them from light, dust, and pets.

If you must fold your quilts, never store them in plastic bags, which can trap harmful moisture. Use clean cotton pillowcases instead. You also want to avoid direct contact with wood, as the oils can leach out into the fabric. To form a protective barrier, line shelves or trunks with clean cotton sheets, lengths of muslin, or special, acid-free paper.

Another alternative is to store your quilts rolled. A foam pool noodle makes a great core. If that's not an option, create your own noodle by crunching up a long strip of acid-free paper instead.

Roll your quilt around a foam pool noodle for storage.

RESOURCES

AccuQuilt GO! Fabric Cutter and dies

AccuQuilt ▪ accuquilt.com

Appli-kay Wonder Pressure Sensitive Fusible Webbing

Floriani Embroidery ▪
florianisoftware.com/quilters-corner.html

BERNINA sewing machines

BERNINA of America, Inc. ▪ bernina.com

4-in-1 Essential Sewing Tool, Carol Doak's Paper, Vellum, and others

C&T Publishing ▪ ctpub.com

Fray Check

Prym Consumer USA ▪ dritz.com

FriXion pens

Pilot Corporation of America ▪ pilotpen.us

June Tailor Fray Block

June Tailor ▪ junetailor.com

Libby Lehman's The Bottom Line, Alex Anderson's MasterPiece, MonoPoly, and other fine threads

Superior Threads ▪ superiorthreads.com

Quilting supplies

The Cotton Patch ▪ quiltusa.com

Note: Fabric manufacturers discontinue fabrics regularly. Exact fabrics shown may no longer be available.

Ricky Tims' Stable Stuff Poly

Ricky Tims, Inc. ▪ rickytims.com

Sewer's Fix-It Tape

Nancy's Notions ▪ nancysnotions.com

Sewline Fabric Glue Pen

Westek Incorporated ▪ sewline-product.com

Synthrapol and Retayne

Pro Chemical and Dye ▪ prochemicalanddye.com

505 Spray and Fix Temporary Fabric Adhesive

ODIF USA ▪ odifusa.com

To contact other designers with work appearing in this book:

Sue Garman / Come Quilt ▪ comequilt.com

Linda Jenkins (& Becky Goldsmith) /
Piece O' Cake ▪ pieceocake.com

Cindy Needham ▪ cindyneedham.com

Sandy Klop/American Jane Patterns ▪ americanjane.com
Note: The following quilts—Charming Checks (page 93), Wagon Wheels (page 100), and Pezzy Pizzaz (page 101)— are available as patterns from American Jane Patterns.

Alex Anderson's love affair with quiltmaking began in 1978, when she completed her Grandmother's Flower Garden quilt as part of her work toward a degree in art at San Francisco State University. Over the years, her focus has rested on understanding fabric relationships and on an intense appreciation for traditional quilting surface design and star quilts.

Alex's mission statement is to educate, inspire, entertain, and grow today's quilting community. With these goals in mind (and action), she has had the privilege and pleasure of ushering tens of thousands of new people into the world of quilting. For eleven years, she hosted television's premier quilt show, *Simply Quilts*, and she is currently the cohost and an executive producer of *The Quilt Show with Ricky Tims* (thequiltshow.com), an interactive website featuring full production videos that is connecting quilters worldwide.

When Alex is not traveling, she resides in Northern California with her husband, her kitty, and the challenges of feeding various forms of wildlife in her backyard. Visit her website at alexandersonquilts.com.

Other products by Alex Anderson:

Also available as an eBook

Also available as an eBook

Also available as an eBook

Also available as an eBook

Also available as an eBook

Also available as an eBook

Also available as an eBook

Also available as an enhanced eBook

Also available as an eBook

Also available as an eBook

Great Titles and Products

from C&T PUBLISHING and stashBOOKS.

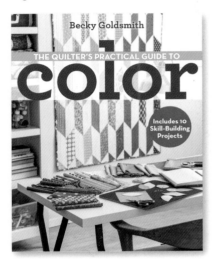

Available at your local retailer or **ctpub.com** *or* **800-284-1114**

For a list of other fine books from C&T Publishing, visit our website
to view our catalog online.

C&T PUBLISHING, INC.
P.O. Box 1456
Lafayette, CA 94549
800-284-1114

Email: ctinfo@ctpub.com
Website: ctpub.com

Tips and Techniques can be found at ctpub.com/quilting-sewing-tips.

For quilting supplies:

COTTON PATCH
1025 Brown Ave.
Lafayette, CA 94549
Store: 925-284-1177
Mail order: 925-283-7883

Email: CottonPa@aol.com
Website: quiltusa.com

Note: Fabrics shown may not be currently available, as fabric
manufacturers keep most fabrics in print for only a short time.